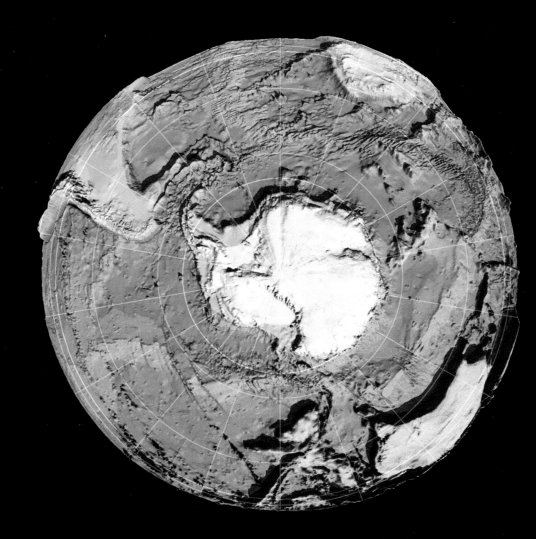

SOUTHERN HEMISPHERE

A DK PUBLISHING BOOK

PROJECT EDITOR/DESIGNER: Wim Jenkins

PROJECT DESIGNERS: Paul Williams, Carol Ann Davis

TERRAIN MODELS PRODUCED IN DK CARTOPIA BY: Rob Stokes

CARTOGRAPHERS: James Anderson, Martin Darlison

INDEX–GAZETTEER: Julia Lynch

US EDITOR: William Lach

SENIOR CARTOGRAPHIC EDITOR: Roger Bullen

MANAGING EDITOR: Lisa Thomas

SENIOR MANAGING ART EDITOR: Philip Lord

PRODUCTION: David Proffit

First American Edition, 1998
4 6 8 10 9 7 5 3
Published in the United States by DK Publishing, Inc.
95 Madison Avenue, New York, New York 10016

Visit us on the World Wide Web at http://www.dk.com

Library of Congress Cataloging-in-Publication Data
The Ultimate Panoramic Atlas. —1st American ed.
    p. cm.
Shows 3-D topography of mountain ranges and the ocean floor.
ISBN 0-7894-3423-7
    1. Atlases.
G1021 .U43   1998   <G&M>
912–DC21
                                                    98-7725
                                                    CIP
                                                    MAPS

Reprographics by Kilographics, London
Printed and bound in Italy by: L.E.G.O., Vicenza

CONTENTS

HOW PANORAMAS WORK 2

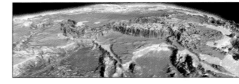
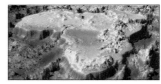

THE
ULTIMATE
PANORAMIC
ATLAS

DK Publishing, Inc.

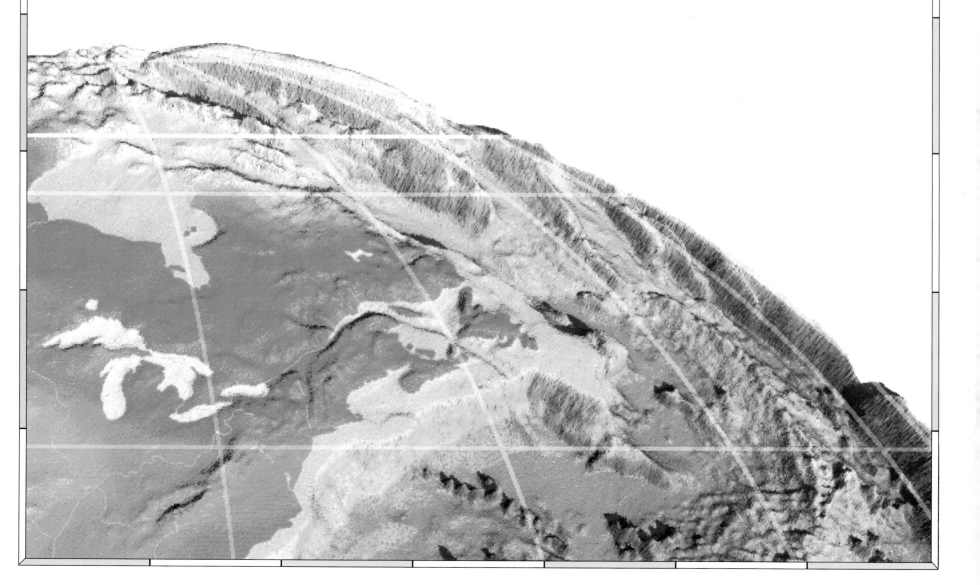

NORTH
AMERICA

HUDSON
BAY

ROCKY MOUNTAINS

GREAT
LAKES

GREAT PLAINS

ALEUTIAN TRENCH

WEST INDIES

HAWAII

PACIFIC
OCEAN

ANDES

EAST PACIFIC RISE

PATAGONIA

ANTARCTIC PENI

How Panoramas Work

THIS ATLAS GIVES AN ENTIRELY NEW VIEW of the world. Topographic data was central to plotting the maps, which were then exaggerated using the latest computer technology. The result – known as a terrain model – presents a very different kind of geography than that of other atlases. Here, the loftiest mountain peaks and the deepest ocean trenches are visible as never before.

③ MAKING THE TERRAIN MODEL

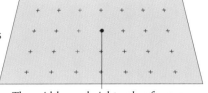

Height values are joined to create a wire frame model.

When the grid information has been fed into the computer, it can be transformed into a simple terrain model known as a "wire frame model." The individual height points are joined together with lines, to give a three-dimensional picture of the Earth's surface.

① THE LAND HEIGHT GRID

All of the Earth's surface – on land and under the ocean – has been divided up into a series of points on a grid. Every point on the grid has an accurate height value. The grid forms the framework for the terrain model.

The grid has a height value for every mile on the Earth's surface.

④ COVERING THE WIRE FRAME

An artificial light source emphasizes mountains and valleys.

To make the model even more realistic, a smooth surface is created. Then the computer uses an artificial light source to give the effect of light and shadow on hills and mountains so that they can be more clearly seen.

② ADDING DETAIL

More detailed information about the surface of the land – such as the altitude of every hill, mountain, valley, and ocean depth – is added to the terrain model. This creates a much more detailed grid.

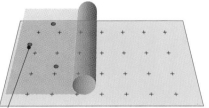

These points record the individual heights of hills, mountains, and valleys.

⑤ COLORING THE MAP

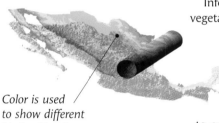

Color is used to show different kinds of land use.

Information about the coastline, vegetation, and land use, compiled using both satellite imagery and ground survey information, is then scanned into the computer. This is placed over the hill shading, to create a fully colored 3-D map.

The height of these mountains has been exaggerated by two and a half times.

Satellite photographs of the Earth's surface are used to create realistic colors for the landscape.

Shadows emphasize the depth of valleys and ocean troughs as well as the height of mountains.

The shelves on which the continents rest are clearly shown.

Desert

Continental slope

Mountain ranges and deep troughs are revealed beneath the ocean.

By highlighting exceptional features of the landscape, the panorama creates a dramatic picture of the Earth's surface.

⑥ MAKING THE MAP INTO A PANORAMA

When the terrain model is complete, the computer can stretch the model in any direction. By exaggerating the scale of the height data, mountains appear more clearly. And by using the computer to create a wide view of the landscape, a panorama is created, as if the Earth were being viewed from space.

Ocean trench

CENTRAL
SIBERIAN
PLATEAU

WEST
SIBERIAN
PLAIN

S I B E R I A

A S I A

PLATEAU
OF TIBET

GOBI

KAMCHATKA

HIMALAYAS

JAPAN

DECCAN

PACIFIC
OCEAN

PHILIPPINES

SUMATRA

BORNEO

NEW GUINEA

NINETYEAST RIDGE

JAVA

INDIAN
OCEAN

AUSTRALIA

NEW ZEALAND

SOUTHEAST INDIAN RIDGE

A N T A R C T I C A

5

islands is rocky, mountainous
...ores are frozen into the vast raft
...ches northward to the North Pole.

8,543 ft

ELLESMERE
ISLAND

GREENLAND

Greenland is covered by a sheet of ice more than 4,900 ft deep,
which means that on average, Greenland is higher than the
Rocky Mountains. The ice is so heavy that it has pushed the
center of the island down below the surrounding ocean.

BAFFIN ISLAND

FOXE BASIN

HUDSON BAY

Hudson Bay is the world's largest bay. Its shoreline
is 12,265 mi long – two and a half times the
distance from New York to San Francisco.

PÉNINSULE
D' UNGAVA

GREAT SLAVE LAKE
is one of thousands of smaller lakes
dotted across this part of the continent.
The lakes were formed as ice sheets melted
at the end of the last Ice Age.

C A N A D I A N   S H I E L D

LAKE
WINNIPEG

JAMES
BAY

GREAT LAKES

The Great Lakes are very shallow. They were
gouged out of the bedrock by powerful glaciers
during the last Ice Age, 20,000 years ago.
When the ice melted, they filled with water.

HARNEY PEAK
+7,241 ft

MOUNT ELBERT
+ 14,432 ft

BLACK
HILLS

Mississippi

Denver
nestles at the foot of
the Rocky Mountains

GREAT PLAINS

At the foot of the Rocky Mountains,
the land flattens out into the Great Plains
– a vast open landscape used for herding
cattle and growing huge crops of wheat.

Missouri

Chicago

Ohio

APPALACHIAN
MOUNTAINS

These ancient peaks were
formed 400 million years ag...
when North America and
Europe were joined as part ...
a supercontinent. Since tho...
time they have eroded and
become worn down.

OZARK PLATEAU

Arkansas

MISSISSIPPI RIVER

The Mississippi–Missouri River system
is the largest in North America, draining
over an eighth of the continent.

SIERRA MADRE ORIENTAL

EDWARDS
PLATEAU

New Orleans

MISSISSIPPI RIVER DELTA

Mud and sand washed downstream by the Mississippi
River has formed a large delta that juts out into the Gulf
of Mexico. The sediment is gradually filling it in.

Mexico City
is one of the world's highest
cities, resting in a valle...
surrounded by mountains.

VOLCÁN PICO
DE ORIZABA
+ 18,701 ft

METEOR STRIKE

65 million years ago, a huge meteor hit the earth here,
forming a crater 190 mi across. Debris thrown into the
atmosphere altered our climate so radically that it
could have caused the extinction of the dinosaurs.

CERRO
ZEMPOALTEPEC
+ 11,138 ft

YUC...
PEN...

SIERRA MADRE DEL SUR

S I E R R A

MIDDLE AMERICA TRENCH

❶ OLD VOLCANOES

The Aleutians are a thin arc of volcanic islands that extend from North America toward Russia. They are a part of the Pacific "Ring of Fire" - a string of mountains and active volcanoes that surrounds the Pacific Ocean.

❻ ICY PEAKS

At the tip of the Canadian arcti
Ellesmere Island. Its northern s
of permanent pack ice that stre

❶

ALEUTIAN ISLANDS

MACKENZIE MOUNTAINS

MOUNT MCKINLEY
(DENALI)
North America's highest
point is 20,322 ft high.

MOUNT ST. HELENS
On May 18th, 1981, Mount
St. Helens erupted, sending an
enormous mud and rock slide down
the mountain at 155 mph.
It causes devastated 212 sq mi
of surrounding forest.

PATTON
SEAMOUNT

ALEUTIAN TRENCH

SAN
JOAQUIN
VALLEY

SIERRA NEVADA

❸

GREAT
BASIN

COLORADO
PLATEAU

GRAND
CANYON

San Francisco
lies on the San Andreas
Fault and has been
hit by many violent
earthquakes.

TUFTS PLAIN

+ -10,663 ft

❷

MENDOCINO FRACTURE ZONE

GULF OF CALIFORNIA

BAJA CALIFORNIA

GUADALUPE

❷ FINGER OF LAND

The thin finger of land extending south into the Pacific Ocean is known as Baja California. It is separated from Mexico by the Gulf of California. The two places are gradually being pulled apart by the spreading of the ocean floor.

❸ JAGGED PEAKS

Massive forces in the Earth pushed up the western side of North America into jagged mountain peaks 80 million years ago. The Rocky Mountains are the highest of the mountains. The Colorado River has carved a deep cleft through the southern mountains, creating the spectacular Grand Canyon.

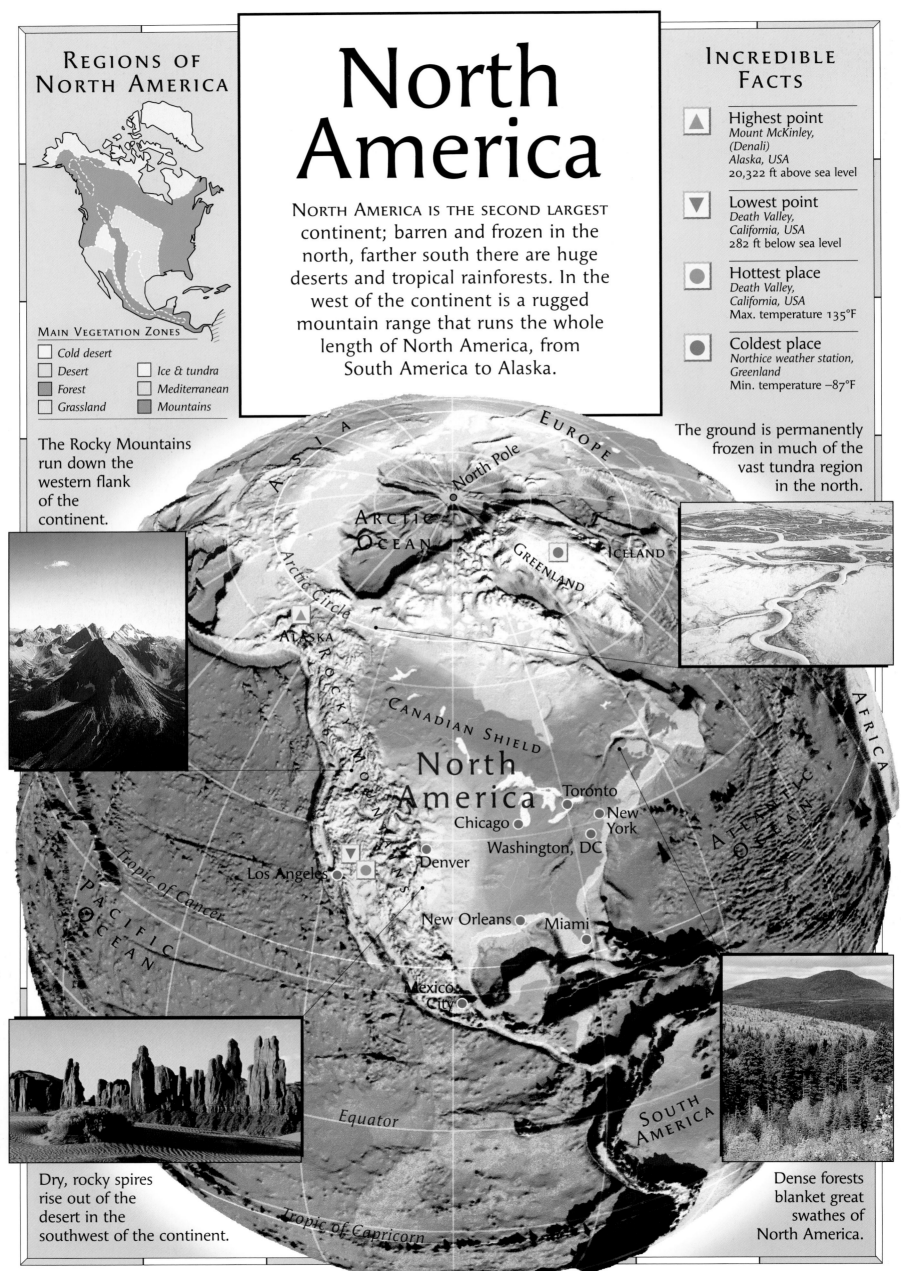

REGIONS OF NORTH AMERICA

MAIN VEGETATION ZONES
- ☐ Cold desert
- ☐ Desert
- ☐ Forest
- ☐ Grassland
- ☐ Ice & tundra
- ☐ Mediterranean
- ☐ Mountains

North America

NORTH AMERICA IS THE SECOND LARGEST continent; barren and frozen in the north, farther south there are huge deserts and tropical rainforests. In the west of the continent is a rugged mountain range that runs the whole length of North America, from South America to Alaska.

INCREDIBLE FACTS

▲ **Highest point**
*Mount McKinley,
(Denali)
Alaska, USA*
20,322 ft above sea level

▼ **Lowest point**
*Death Valley,
California, USA*
282 ft below sea level

● **Hottest place**
*Death Valley,
California, USA*
Max. temperature 135°F

● **Coldest place**
*Northice weather station,
Greenland*
Min. temperature −87°F

The Rocky Mountains run down the western flank of the continent.

The ground is permanently frozen in much of the vast tundra region in the north.

Dry, rocky spires rise out of the desert in the southwest of the continent.

Dense forests blanket great swathes of North America.

6

8,400 mi

North
America

3,400 mi

Pacific
Ocean

SOUTH
AMERICA

⑤ LOW-LYING

Florida is surrounded by shallow seas that cover
the continental shelf. This shelf area was once land,
but became drowned when sea levels rose
after the last Ice Age.

④ SPIKY ISLANDS

The huge spike rising from the ocean
floor is the great volcano that formed
the islands of Bermuda. The smaller
spikes nearby are called
seamounts and lie completely
beneath the ocean.

ICELAND

NORTHWEST ATLANTIC MID-OCEAN CANYON

LAURENTIAN
HIGHLANDS

MONT
JACQUES-CARTIER
+4,160 ft

GULF OF
ST. LAWRENCE

NEWFOUNDLAND

GRAND BANKS
OF NEWFOUNDLAND

TITANIC

In April 1912, the Titanic, sailing on her
maiden voyage, hit an iceberg and sank with the
loss of about 1500 lives. The wreck lies here,
more than 13,000 ft below the ocean's surface.

NOVA
SCOTIA

St. Lawrence River

Toronto

New York ○
lies at the mouth of
the Hudson River

APPALACHIAN
MOUNTAINS

LAURENTIAN FAN
Sediment washed down by
the St. Lawrence River has
formed a huge fan on the
deep ocean floor.

ISLAND COAST
The eastern coast of the USA is
low-lying and has many barrier
islands and spits that are
formed by waves and storms
in the Atlantic Ocean.

④

BERMUDA

NEW ENGLAND
SEAMOUNTS

⑤

THE EVERGLADES
are a huge swampy expanse,
covering much of southern Florida.

FLORIDA

HATTERAS
PLAIN
+ -16,949 ft

BAHAMAS

Miami ○

HISPANIOLA

CUBA
This is the largest of the
Caribbean islands. Most of the
islands in this area were formed
by intense volcanic activity.

JAMAICA

AN
ULA

MADRE

MOUNTAIN BELT
Central America is dominated by several large
mountain chains that are part of the Sierra Madre.
Earthquakes and volcanic eruptions are very
common as the land below is near a boundary in the
earth's crust, where the land is constantly moving.

MOSQUITO
COAST

LAKE NICARAGUA
Two large volcanoes rise out
of the middle of this immense
lake in Central America.

CERRO CHIRRIPÓ
GRANDE
+12,530 ft

ISTHMUS OF PANAMA
The Panama Canal cuts through the Isthmus
of Panama here, to form a link for ships between
the Atlantic and Pacific Oceans.

TRINIDAD

UNT RORAIMA
9,219 ft

UIANA
HLANDS

AMAZON BASIN

The massive forces that formed the Andes caused
the land to buckle and form this huge, shallow
depression. The Amazon River, which flows through
the basin, carries more water to the sea
than any other river in the world.

Amazon

MOUTHS
OF THE AMAZON

PIRANHAS

Vicious piranha fish live in the swampy
waters and rivers of the Amazon Basin.
They hunt in schools and, working as a
team, can strip the flesh off living
creatures in seconds.

ALTIPLANO

The Altiplano is a high plateau
that sits between two chains
of the Andes. It is one of the
highest permanently settled
areas in the world.

CORDILLERA ORIENTAL

CIDENTAL

E

S

ACAMA DESERT

cama Desert, in the shadow
Andes, is the driest place on
's surface. Often it does not
ere for decades at a time.

PLANALTO DE
MATO GROSSO

The Mato Grosso (meaning "Great Forest")
is an old, eroded plateau, covered with a mixture
of rough savanna grasslands and woodland.

GRAN CHACO

The Gran Chaco is a thorny, marshy
scrubland crossed by streams and
rivers that wash sediments
down from the Andes.

Paraguay

CERRO
ACONCAGUA
22,831 ft
South America's
highest point)

SIERRAS DE
CÓRDOBA

A

Paraná

PAMPAS

The Pampas region is home to many
of South America's beef cattle. The name
Pampas is a native Quechua Indian
word meaning "flat plain."

N

E

N

③

JUAN FERNANDEZ
ISLANDS

D

PATAGONIA

a desolate, mountainous are
in southern South America.
Rainfall is scarce and most of
Patagonia is a cold desert.

E

+ -13,228 ft

②

ICY FJORDS

Deep fjords are common in this part
of the continent. They reach deep
into the snow-capped Andes and are
often covered by glaciers flowing
down from the mountains above.

C H I L E   R I S E

o mi
v and
rties,"

s.

CUBA   +   HISPANIOLA   PUERTO RICO

PICO
CRISTÓBAL
CÓLON
18,947 ft

○ Bogotá

ISTHMUS
OF PANAMA

CORDILLERA
ORIENTAL

LLANOS
*is the Spanish term for a
large area of savanna-
like grassland*

M

G
HIG

+ COTOPAXI
19,347 ft

① Guayaquil ○

COCOS RIDGE

CORDILLERA O

CARNEGIE RIDGE

A

N

D

Lima ○

A-
*The At
of the
the Earl
rain*

**① DEEP
TRENCH**

Off the Pacific Coast
of South America, the
sea floor plunges into a
deep trough. Over 3,700
mi long, the Peru–Chile
Trench marks the point
where two parts of
the Earth's crust
meet and collide.

PERU–CHILE TRENCH

PERU
BASIN
+ -16,381 ft

+ -659 ft

+ -3,127 ft

NAZCA RIDGE

CHI
BASI

SAN
AMBROSIO
ISLAND

**② WALL OF
MOUNTAINS**

The huge Andes mountain
range runs all the way down
the Pacific Coast. Its high peaks
are being forced higher and
higher all the time as South
America collides with the floor
of the Pacific Ocean. Many of
the mountains are volcanoes,
and some of the world's largest
volcanoes, such as Cotopaxi,
are found here.

SALA Y GOMEZ RIDGE

ROGGEVEEN
BASIN

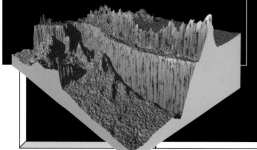

**③ CASTAWAY
ISLANDS**

The Juan Fernandez Islands lie 400 mi west
of the coast of Chile. The islands were formed by
volcanoes and rise steeply from a ridge on the
ocean floor. *Robinson Crusoe* was based on the
story of Alexander Selkirk, who was shipwrecked
on these remote islands.

④ ICE AND SNOW

The southern tip of South America is only 56
away from Antarctica, and the land there is ic
frozen. Strong westerly winds, the "Roaring Fo
create mountainous seas and make this one
of the world's most treacherous areas for ship

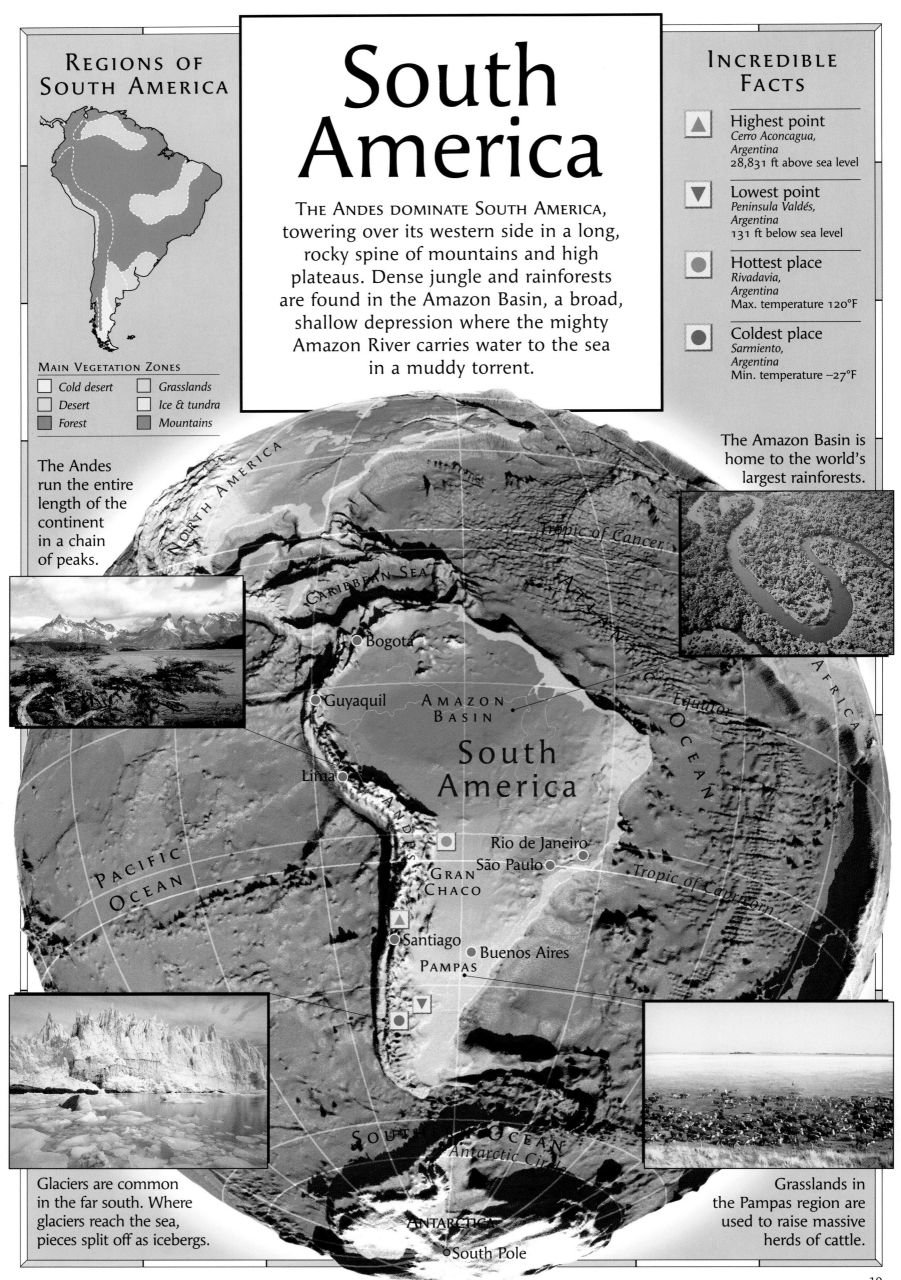

MAIN VEGETATION ZONES

- Cold desert
- Desert
- Forest
- Grasslands
- Ice & tundra
- Mountains

The Andes run the entire length of the continent in a chain of peaks.

South America

THE ANDES DOMINATE SOUTH AMERICA, towering over its western side in a long, rocky spine of mountains and high plateaus. Dense jungle and rainforests are found in the Amazon Basin, a broad, shallow depression where the mighty Amazon River carries water to the sea in a muddy torrent.

INCREDIBLE FACTS

▲ Highest point
Cerro Aconcagua, Argentina
28,831 ft above sea level

▼ Lowest point
Peninsula Valdés, Argentina
131 ft below sea level

◉ Hottest place
Rivadavia, Argentina
Max. temperature 120°F

◉ Coldest place
Sarmiento, Argentina
Min. temperature −27°F

The Amazon Basin is home to the world's largest rainforests.

NORTH AMERICA

Tropic of Cancer

CARIBBEAN SEA

Bogota

Guyaquil

AMAZON BASIN

South America

ATLANTIC OCEAN

AFRICA

Equator

Lima

ANDES

Rio de Janeiro

São Paulo

GRAN CHACO

Tropic of Capricorn

PACIFIC OCEAN

Santiago

Buenos Aires

PAMPAS

SOUTHERN OCEAN

Antarctic Circle

ANTARCTICA

South Pole

Glaciers are common in the far south. Where glaciers reach the sea, pieces split off as icebergs.

Grasslands in the Pampas region are used to raise massive herds of cattle.

6 OLD PLATEAU

The Guiana Highlands are made out of some of the oldest rocks in the world. Ancient, eroded plateaus rise out of the dense rainforest. Rivers that plunge off the edges of these high plateaus have formed large waterfalls such as Angel Falls, the world's highest waterfall, at 3,212 ft high.

Pacific Ocean

South America

Atlantic Ocean

ANTARCTICA

PLANALTO DA BORBOREMA

BRAZILIAN HIGHLANDS

The Brazilian Highlands are a series of valleys and plateaus. The old rocks have been heavily worn down and eroded.

+ -19,501 ft

BRAZIL BASIN

ILHAS MARTIN VAZ

São Paulo

is South America's largest metropolis and the world's third largest city.

Rio de Janeiro

sits at the edge of Guanabara Bay, which acts as a huge natural harbor, sheltering the city from the Atlantic Ocean.

+ -285 ft

TRINDADE SPUR

SANTOS PLATEAU

+ -2,993 ft

RIO GRANDE RISE

Buenos Aires

RÍO DE LA PLATA

RIO GRANDE GAP

5 SHALLOW SEAS

The sparsely inhabited Falkland Islands sit on an extension of the continental shelf, surrounded by relatively shallow seas. The islands are held by the United Kingdom. In 1982, an ongoing dispute about their ownership between Argentina and the United Kingdom resulted in the Falklands War.

+ -331 ft

ARGENTINE BASIN

+ -19,619 ft

GULF OF SAN JORGE

5

TIERRA DEL FUEGO

was given its name (meaning "Land of Fire") by European explorers, who saw fires lining the shores, lit by the native people.

FALKLAND ISLANDS

FALKLAND PLATEAU

4

STRAIT OF MAGELLAN

BURDWOOD BANK

CAPE HORN

is the southernmost tip of South America. It was named "Hoorn" after the birthplace of the Dutch navigator Willem Corneliszoon Schouten, who rounded it in 1616.

OB'
BANK

SPITSBERGEN

FRAN
JOSE
LAND

*een, as its
Norwegian
years, named
settle there.*

JAN MAYEN

ICE SHEET
*A huge 9,800 ft thick ice sheet sat on
top of Scandinavia and much of
northern Europe during the last Ice
Age, 18,000 years ago. The weight of
the ice pushed the land down. Once
the ice melted, the land began to rise.
Scandinavia is still rising, in some
places by almost 4 inches a year.*

−1,230 ft

BARENTS
TROUGH

MURMANS
RISE

ICELAND
PLATEAU

JAN MAYEN RIDGE

MOHNS RIDGE

NORWEGIAN BASIN

LAPLAND

SCANDINAVIAN
SHIELD

⑥

GALDHØPIGGEN
+8,100 ft

S C A N D I N A V I A

GULF OF BOTHNIA

St. Petersburg

*This area of northern Europe contains som
of the continent's oldest rocks. It was
scraped and scoured by glaciers, which le
a flat, marshy landscape when they melte*

FAEROE
ISLANDS

SHETLAND
ISLANDS

Stockholm

GULF OF FINLAND

NORTH SEA
*The North Sea is very shallow.
During the last Ice Age, when sea
levels were lower, it formed a "land
bridge" between the British Isles
and the rest of Europe.*

+
−164 ft

JYLLAND

BALTIC
SEA

NORTH EUROPEAN PLAIN
*The North European Plain is one of the
world's largest continual expanses
of flat land. It extends from the
English Channel to the Urals.*

N O R T H   E U R O P E A N   P L A I N

Rhine

Berlin

③

Elbe

Oder

Vistula

MONT BLANC
+15,771 ft

A L P S

Po

Venice lies on an island in the
middle of a lagoon. The whole
city is gradually sinking, and
Venice is often flooded.

TATRA
MOUNTAINS

CARPATHIAN
MOUNTAINS

GREAT
HUNGARIAN
PLAIN

Danube

TRANSYLVANIAN ALPS

ITALIAN
PENINSULA

Venice

CORNO GRANDE
+9,560 ft

DINARIC ALPS

Danube

APENNINES

BALKAN MOUNTAINS

CORSICA

Rome

ADRIATIC
SEA

SARDINIA

TYRRHENIAN
SEA

AEGEAN SEA
*The small islands dotted
across the Aegean Sea are
the tops of old mountains
that became submerged
when the sea floor
subsided.*

SICILY

Athens

PELOPONNESE

VESUVIUS
*Vesuvius is mainland Europe's only active
volcano. Its most devastating eruption
was in A.D. 79, when a massive ash cloud
literally buried the ancient towns
of Pompeii and Herculaneum.*

M E D I T E R R A N E A N   S E A

GOLFE DE
GABÈS

MALTA

IONIAN
BASIN

−11,503 ft +

CRETE

(1) ISLAND OF ICE AND FIRE

Iceland is a rugged island in the Atlantic Ocean. It has both icy glaciers and fiery volcanoes. This is because it sits directly over the Reykjanes Ridge, a large crack in the Earth's crust and a part of the Mid-Atlantic Ridge, which runs all the way up the Atlantic Ocean. In 1996, a volcano erupted beneath Iceland's largest glacier, melting the ice and causing a massive flood.

GREENLAND

Greenland is the world's largest island and not g[...] name suggests, but white and icy. In AD 982 the[...] Erik the Red, who had been banished there for thre[...] it "Greenland" in an effort to encourage people to[...]

(1)

HVANNADALSHNÚKU[...]
+6,952 ft

ICELAND

EIRIK RIDGE

REYKJANES BASIN
−11,024 ft +

REYKJANES RIDGE

ICELAND BASIN

HATTON RIDGE

FENI RIDGE

(2)

BEN NEVIS
+4,406 ft

BRITISH ISLES

CHARLIE–GIBBS FRACTURE ZONE

IRELAND

BRITAIN

(2) GREEN ISLANDS

Two large islands and many smaller islands lie just off the west coast of mainland Europe. They are known as the British Isles and sit on the continental shelf, surrounded by relatively shallow seas.

PORCUPINE BANK

CELTIC SHELF

London

Swirling ocean currents and frequent storms make this a hazardous area for ships.

ENGLISH CHANNEL

PORCUPINE PLAIN

LOIRE

BAY OF BISCAY

Paris

was founded over 2,000 years ago on an island in the middle of the Seine river.

CORDILLERA CANTÁBRICA

ANETO
+11,168 ft

MASSIF CENTRAL

PYRENEES

The mountains of the Pyrenees form a lofty barrier between the Iberian Peninsula and the rest of Europe.

Madrid ○

IBERIAN PENINSULA

IBERIAN PLAIN

BALEARIC ISLANDS

ALGER[...] BASI[...]

+9,15[...]

SIERRA NEVADA

STRAIT OF GIBRALTAR

MEDITERRANEAN SEA

The Mediterranean Sea was a hot, dry basin before the Atlantic Ocean breached the narrow Strait of Gibraltar in a huge flood of water. A great waterfall formed as the water started to fill up the Mediterranean basin, a process that took almost a thousand years to complete.

(3) JAGGED MOUNTAINS

The Alps are Europe's tallest and most jagged mountains Their spiky, snow-topped peaks were formed 65 million years ago, when Africa collided with Europe.

AFRICA

EUROPE IS THE WORLD'S SECOND smallest continent. It occupies the western tip of the large landmass known as Eurasia. In the north there are old, eroded mountains, while farther south is the vast, flat North European Plain and much younger, more jagged mountains such as the Alps.

REGIONS OF EUROPE

MAIN VEGETATION ZONES

- Forest
- Grassland
- Ice & tundra
- Mediterranean
- Mountains

INCREDIBLE FACTS

▲ **Highest point**
El'brus,
Russian Federation
18,510 ft above sea level

▼ **Lowest point**
Caspian Depression,
Russian Federation
92 ft below sea level

◉ **Hottest place**
Seville,
Spain
Max. temperature 122°F

◉ **Coldest place**
Ust 'Shchugor,
Russian Federation
Min. temperature −67°F

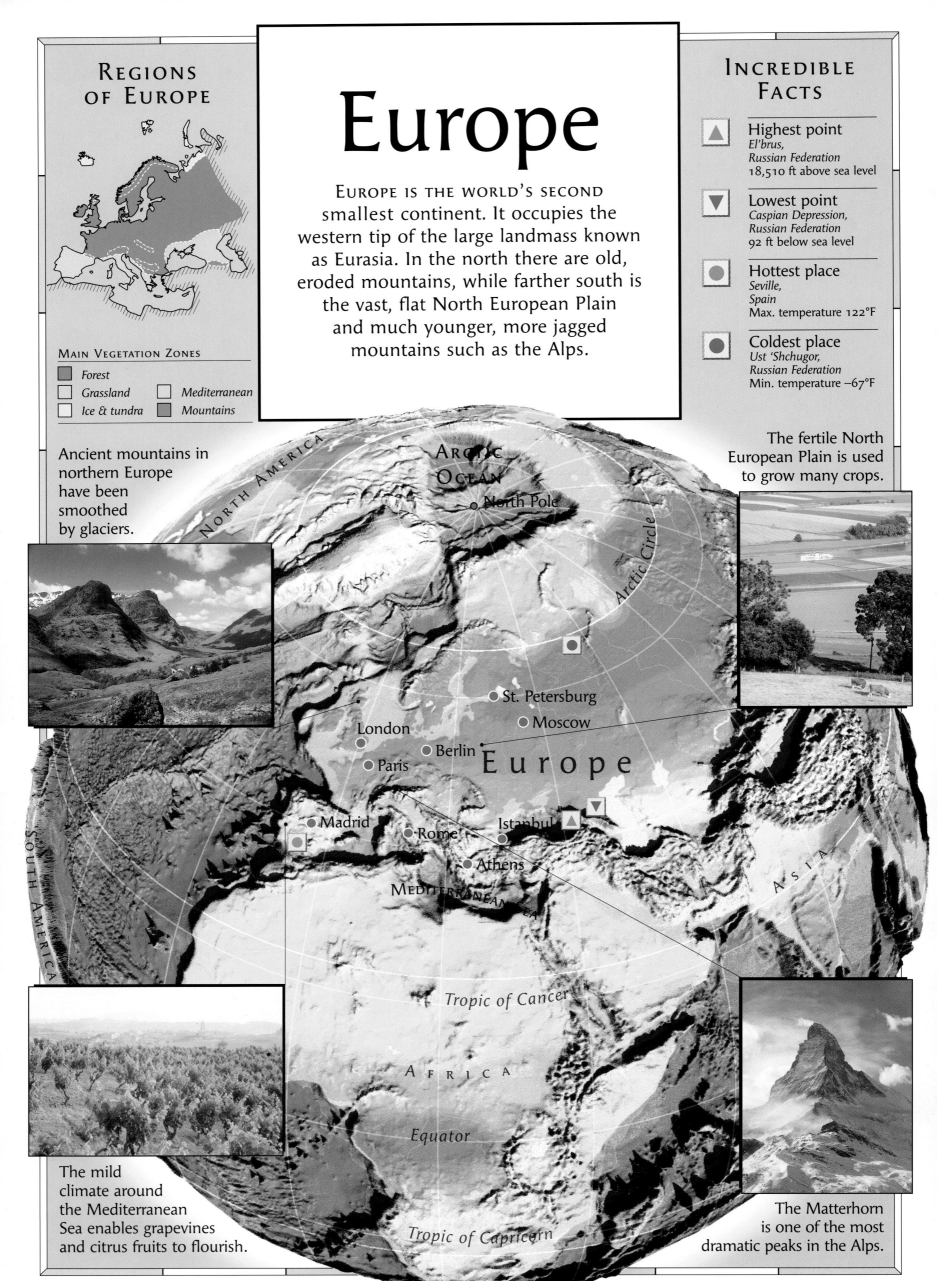

Ancient mountains in northern Europe have been smoothed by glaciers.

The fertile North European Plain is used to grow many crops.

The mild climate around the Mediterranean Sea enables grapevines and citrus fruits to flourish.

The Matterhorn is one of the most dramatic peaks in the Alps.

ARCTIC OCEAN

NORTH AMERICA

North Pole

Arctic Circle

St. Petersburg

Moscow

London

Berlin

Paris

E u r o p e

Madrid

Rome

Istanbul

Athens

MEDITERRANEAN SEA

ASIA

SOUTH AMERICA

Tropic of Cancer

A F R I C A

Equator

Tropic of Capricorn

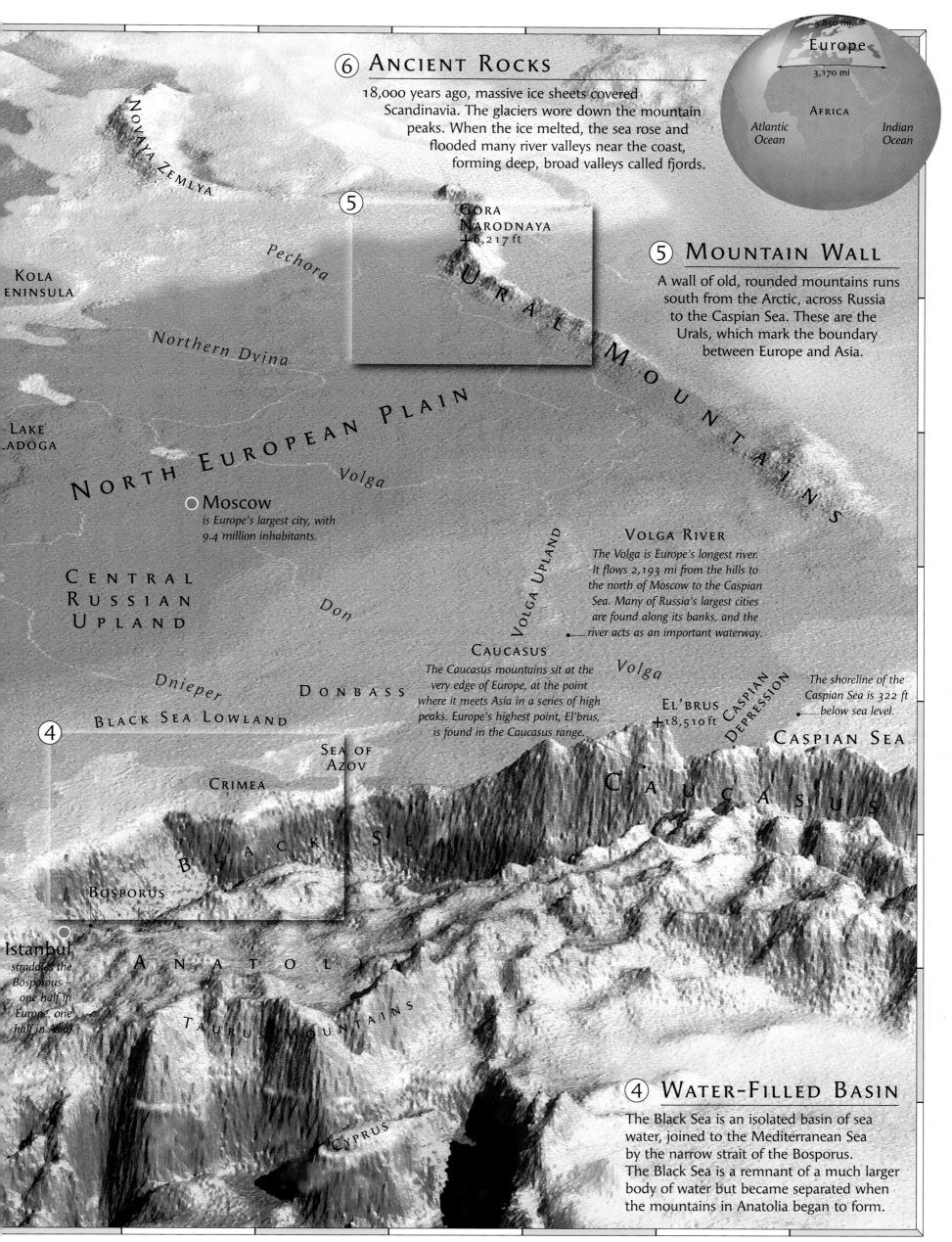

⑥ ANCIENT ROCKS

18,000 years ago, massive ice sheets covered Scandinavia. The glaciers wore down the mountain peaks. When the ice melted, the sea rose and flooded many river valleys near the coast, forming deep, broad valleys called fjords.

Europe

3,850 mi
3,170 mi

AFRICA

Atlantic
Ocean

Indian
Ocean

NOVAYA ZEMLYA

⑤

GORA
NARODNAYA
+6,217 ft

Pechora

KOLA
ENINSULA

U R A L   M O U N T A I N S

⑤ MOUNTAIN WALL

A wall of old, rounded mountains runs south from the Arctic, across Russia to the Caspian Sea. These are the Urals, which mark the boundary between Europe and Asia.

Northern Dvina

N O R T H   E U R O P E A N   P L A I N

-LAKE
ADOGA

Volga

○ MOSCOW
is Europe's largest city, with
9.4 million inhabitants.

VOLGA RIVER

The Volga is Europe's longest river. It flows 2,193 mi from the hills to the north of Moscow to the Caspian Sea. Many of Russia's largest cities are found along its banks, and the river acts as an important waterway.

C E N T R A L
R U S S I A N
U P L A N D

Don

VOLGA UPLAND

CAUCASUS

The Caucasus mountains sit at the very edge of Europe, at the point where it meets Asia in a series of high peaks. Europe's highest point, El'brus, is found in the Caucasus range.

Volga

EL'BRUS
+18,510 ft

CASPIAN
DEPRESSION

The shoreline of the Caspian Sea is 322 ft below sea level.

Dnieper

D O N B A S S

BLACK SEA LOWLAND

④

SEA OF
AZOV

CRIMEA

CASPIAN SEA

C A U C A S U S

B L A C K   S E A

BOSPORUS

Istanbul
straddles the
Bosporous –
one half in
Europe, one
half in Asia)

A N A T O L I A

TAURUS MOUNTAINS

④ WATER-FILLED BASIN

The Black Sea is an isolated basin of sea water, joined to the Mediterranean Sea by the narrow strait of the Bosporus. The Black Sea is a remnant of a much larger body of water but became separated when the mountains in Anatolia began to form.

CYPRUS

GREENLAND

FROZEN OVER

Rivers in northern Siberia frequently freeze over completely. When the spring thaw arrives, the mouths of the rivers are often still blocked with ice, causing floods.

SCANDINAVIA

GORA NARODNAYA
+ 6,217 ft

NORTH EUROPEAN PLAIN

URAL MOUNTAINS

WEST SIBERIAN PLAIN

The West Siberian Plain is an immense, featureless expanse. Much of it is marshy and boggy and crisscrossed by sluggish streams and rivers. Beneath the plain are huge oil and gas reserves.

EL'BRUS
+ 18,510 m

KIRGHIZ STEPPE

CAUCA

CASPIAN DEPRESSION
CAVIAR

The eggs of sturgeon fish caught in the Caspian Sea provide some of the world's most expensive caviar.

CASPIAN SEA

ARAL SEA

DRYING UP

The Aral Sea is rapidly drying up because the rivers that feed it are being diverted to irrigate crops.

K
28,251 ft

TURAN LOWLAND

KARA KUM

HINDU KUSH

Tehran

ZAGROS MOUNTAINS

IRANIAN PLATEAU

KHYBER PASS
+ 3,543 ft

KUH—E TAFTĀN
+ 13,261 ft

DASHT—E—LUT

High winds have worn away the sandstone rocks here to form bare rocky desert surfaces.

SULAIMAN RANGE

Indus

THAR DESERT

The Khyber Pass forms a narrow precipitous route across the mountains. Throughout history, it has been used by invading forces to enter the Indian subcontinent from the northwest.

Delhi

STRAIT OF HORMUZ

GULF OF OMAN

Karachi

Karachi was founded at the edge of a large natural harbor, which protects the city from monsoon storms.

ty quarter"
ontinuous
largely
ed.

+ −955 ft

INDUS FAN

DECCAN

Both the Deccan, a large plateau, and the Arabian Peninsula contain very old eroded rocks. They are remnants of the ancient supercontinent Gondwanaland

Bombay

is one of the largest and most densely populated cities in the world.

RACTURE ZONE

ARABIAN BASIN
+ −13,648 ft

WESTERN GHATS

ANAI MUD
+ 8,842

CHAGOS—LACCADIVE PLATEAU

⑤ MIGHTY RIVERS

The Ganges and Brahmaputra rivers flow from the Himalayas to the Bay of Bengal. Soil and mud is washed downstream and has formed a huge delta. Deposits have also been washed out into the sea, forming a vast underwater mud fan called the Ganges Fan.

② CRACKING UP

The narrow Red Sea divides Africa from Asia. On the seabed, there is a large crack, or rift, which is gradually opening up, causing Africa and Asia to split apart.

① ROOF OF THE WORLD

The mountains of the Himalayas tower above the Indian subcontinent and contain Mount Everest, the world's highest peak. They were created as the Indian landmass rammed into the rest of Asia, crumpling up the land. The great tableland of the Plateau of Tibet lies to the north, with the cold, desert-filled Tarim Basin at its northern edge.

BRITISH ISLE

ALPS

ANATOLIA ④

MEDITERRANEAN SEA

MESOPOTAMIA

Tigris

AFRICA

SYRIAN DESERT

OIL

Baghdad ○

The world's richest oil deposits lie beneath the Gulf. Over a quarter of all the world's oil is produced here.

Euphrates

②

③

RED SEA

ASIR

○ Mecca

Mecca is the birthplace of the prophet Muhammad, founder of Islam. It is the holiest city in the Islamic world, and Muslims strive to make a once-in-a-lifetime pilgrimage, called the hajj, to the city.

ARABIAN PENINSULA

THE GULF

JABAL AN NABĪ SHU'AYB
+ 12,041 ft

AR RUB' AL KHALI

EMPTY QUARTE

The Ar Rub' al Khali means "emp in Arabic. It is the largest area of sand in the world and remain unexplored and uninhabi

GULF OF ADEN

SOCOTRA

HORN OF AFRICA

OWEN F

CARLSBERG RIDGE

③ ENDLESS SAND

Most of the Arabian Peninsula is covered by sandy desert. The climate here is very hot and dry, and water is scarce. Towns and villages are often built near oases, places where water from underground springs rises to the surface.

④ SHALLOW SEA

The Gulf divides the mountainous Iranian Plateau from the desert swathes of the Arabian Peninsula. The Tigris and Euphrates rivers empty into the Gulf, after flowing through Mesopotamia, one of the heartlands of human civilization.

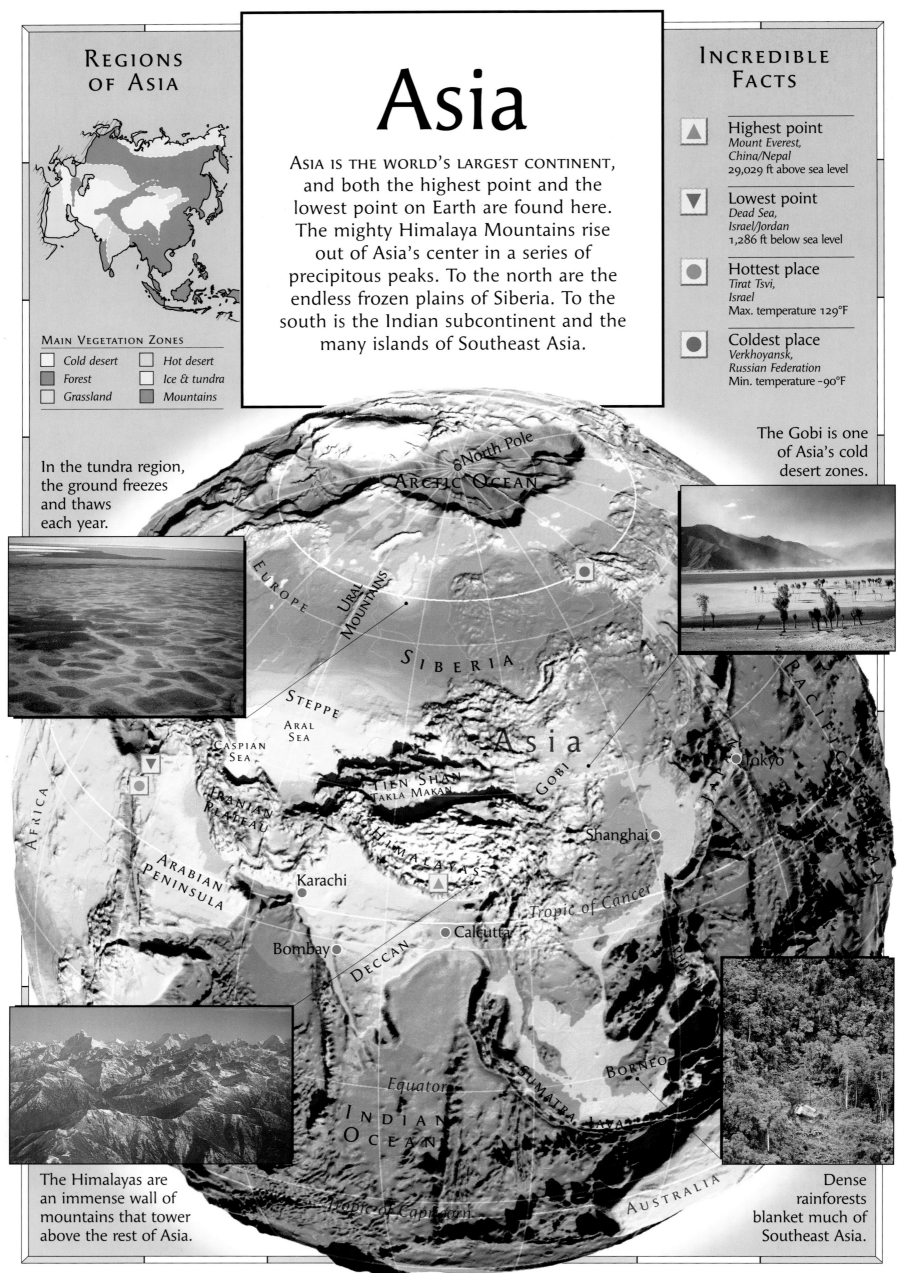

REGIONS OF ASIA

MAIN VEGETATION ZONES

- ☐ Cold desert
- ☐ Forest
- ☐ Grassland
- ☐ Hot desert
- ☐ Ice & tundra
- ☐ Mountains

Asia

ASIA IS THE WORLD'S LARGEST CONTINENT, and both the highest point and the lowest point on Earth are found here. The mighty Himalaya Mountains rise out of Asia's center in a series of precipitous peaks. To the north are the endless frozen plains of Siberia. To the south is the Indian subcontinent and the many islands of Southeast Asia.

INCREDIBLE FACTS

▲ **Highest point**
Mount Everest,
China/Nepal
29,029 ft above sea level

▼ **Lowest point**
Dead Sea,
Israel/Jordan
1,286 ft below sea level

◉ **Hottest place**
Tirat Tsvi,
Israel
Max. temperature 129°F

◉ **Coldest place**
Verkhoyansk,
Russian Federation
Min. temperature -90°F

The Gobi is one of Asia's cold desert zones.

In the tundra region, the ground freezes and thaws each year.

The Himalayas are an immense wall of mountains that tower above the rest of Asia.

Dense rainforests blanket much of Southeast Asia.

Map labels: North Pole, ARCTIC OCEAN, EUROPE, URAL MOUNTAINS, SIBERIA, STEPPE, ARAL SEA, CASPIAN SEA, IRANIAN PLATEAU, ARABIAN PENINSULA, Karachi, Bombay, DECCAN, Calcutta, TIEN SHAN, TAKLA MAKAN, HIMALAYAS, GOBI, Asia, Shanghai, Tokyo, JAPAN, PACIFIC, PHILIPPINES, BORNEO, SUMATRA, JAVA, INDIAN OCEAN, Equator, Tropic of Cancer, Tropic of Capricorn, AUSTRALIA, AFRICA

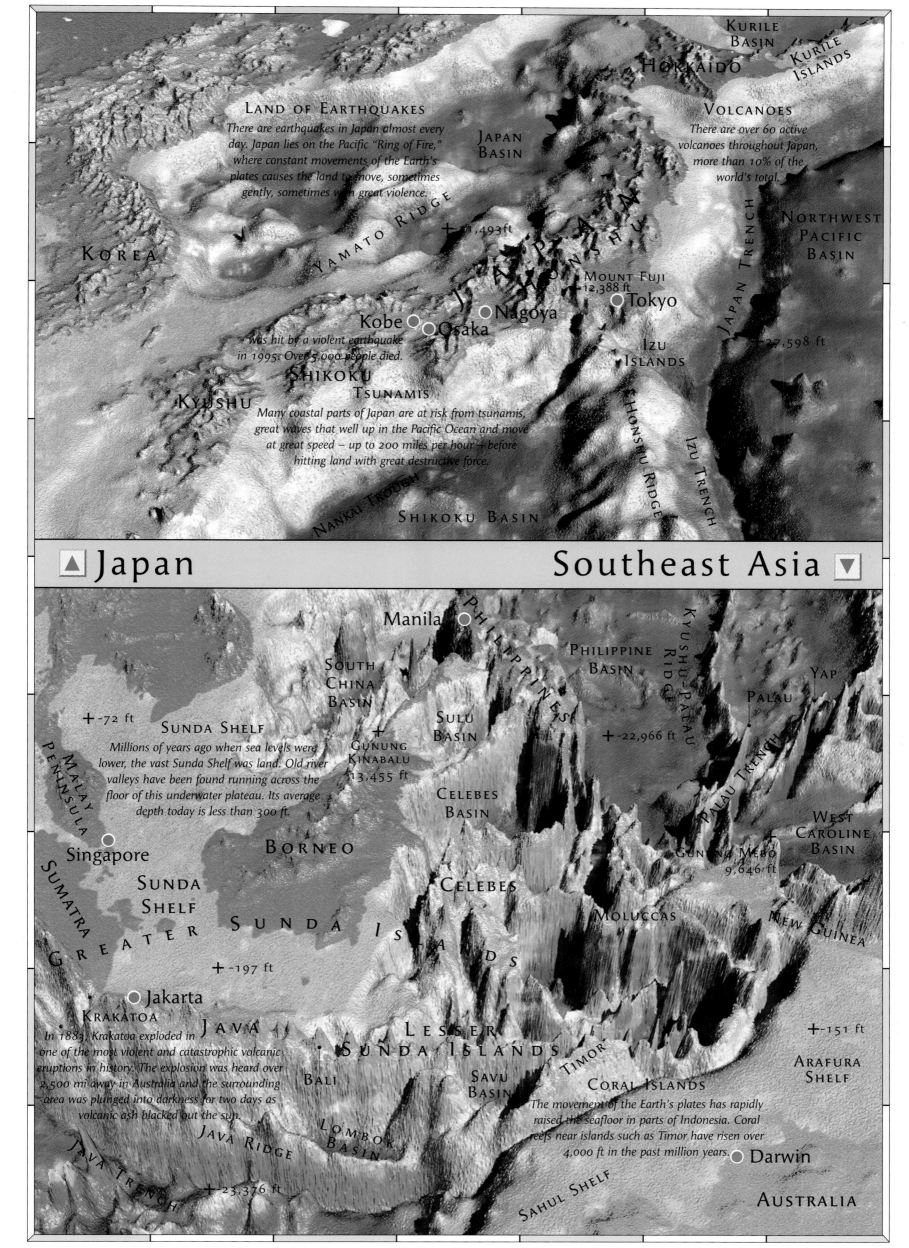

LAND OF EARTHQUAKES

There are earthquakes in Japan almost every day. Japan lies on the Pacific "Ring of Fire," where constant movements of the Earth's plates causes the land to move, sometimes gently, sometimes with great violence.

JAPAN BASIN

KURILE BASIN

HOKKAIDO

KURILE ISLANDS

VOLCANOES

There are over 60 active volcanoes throughout Japan, more than 10% of the world's total.

KOREA

YAMATO RIDGE

+ 27,493ft

JAPAN

HONSHU

NORTHWEST PACIFIC BASIN

JAPAN TRENCH

MOUNT FUJI
12,388 ft

Tokyo

Kobe

Osaka

Nagoya

+ 27,598 ft

was hit by a violent earthquake in 1995. Over 5,000 people died.

IZU ISLANDS

SHIKOKU

KYUSHU

HONSHU RIDGE

IZU TRENCH

TSUNAMIS

Many coastal parts of Japan are at risk from tsunamis, great waves that well up in the Pacific Ocean and move at great speed – up to 200 miles per hour – before hitting land with great destructive force.

NANKAI TROUGH

SHIKOKU BASIN

▲ Japan

Southeast Asia ▼

Manila

PHILIPPINES

KYUSHU-PALAU RIDGE

SOUTH CHINA BASIN

PHILIPPINE BASIN

YAP

SULU BASIN

PALAU

+ -72 ft

SUNDA SHELF

Millions of years ago when sea levels were lower, the vast Sunda Shelf was land. Old river valleys have been found running across the floor of this underwater plateau. Its average depth today is less than 300 ft.

+ GUNUNG KINABALU
13,455 ft

+ -22,966 ft

PALAU TRENCH

MALAY PENINSULA

CELEBES BASIN

WEST CAROLINE BASIN

BORNEO

GUNUNG MEBO
9,646 ft

Singapore

SUNDA SHELF

SUNDA

CELEBES

MOLUCCAS

NEW GUINEA

SUMATRA

GREATER

ISLANDS

+ -197 ft

Jakarta

JAVA

LESSER

TIMOR

+ -151 ft

KRAKATOA

SUNDA ISLANDS

CORAL ISLANDS

ARAFURA SHELF

In 1883, Krakatoa exploded in one of the most violent and catastrophic volcanic eruptions in history. The explosion was heard over 2,500 mi away in Australia and the surrounding area was plunged into darkness for two days as volcanic ash blacked out the sun.

BALI

SAVU BASIN

The movement of the Earth's plates has rapidly raised the seafloor in parts of Indonesia. Coral reefs near islands such as Timor have risen over 4,000 ft in the past million years.

JAVA RIDGE

LOMBOK BASIN

Darwin

JAVA TRENCH

+ -23,376 ft

SAHUL SHELF

AUSTRALIA

(8) VOLCANIC PENINSULA

The Kamchatka peninsula sits at the edge of the Pacific "Ring of Fire," the place where several of the Earth's plates collide. The movement of the land generates intense heat, and many active volcanoes and hot springs are found throughout Kamchatka.

(8)

KLYUCHEVSKAYA
SOPKA
+ 15,584 ft

KAMCHATKA

(7) DEEPEST LAKE

Lake Baikal is 5,315 ft deep – the deepest lake on the Earth's surface. It contains about one fifth of the world's fresh water.

CHINA'S SORROW

The Yellow River is known as "China's Sorrow," because it has claimed more lives than any other physical feature on Earth. In 1887, a huge flood killed over a million people.

MANCHURIA

ESERT

of the Earth's it is neither hot old desert with cky surfaces.

Beijing ○

QIN LING

SICHUAN PENDI

Yellow River

GREAT PLAIN OF CHINA

This is the most populated part of China. Parts of it are covered by fine deposits, called loess, that have been washed down by the Yellow River.

YELLOW SEA

JAPAN

Tokyo ○

KOREA

Shanghai ○
is China's largest city and a major center of commerce and industry.

Yangtze

RYUKYU ISLANDS

11,145 ft +

TAIWAN

Xi Jiang

Hong Kong ○
was returned to China in 1997, after 99 years of British control.

HAINAN DAO

LATEAU

FERTILE DELTA

The Irrawaddy delta has been built up from layers of silt, carried downstream from the ountains by the river. The land is very fertile here, nd rice is grown throughout the delta region.

goon

CHAÎNE ANNAMITIQUE

Mekong

PARACEL ISLANDS

NDAMAN BASIN

Bangkok ○

ISTHMUS OF KRA

SHORT CUT

The narrow Isthmus of Kra is only 25 mi wide at its most narrow point. Plans to build a canal across it have been proposed and scrapped many times over the past 150 years.

Ho Chi Minh City ○

+ -72 ft

LONG PENINSULA

Old granite rocks form the backbone of the Malay Peninsula, which extends south for almost 700 miles. Many beautiful beaches are found along its length, and the surrounding seas are dotted by tiny limestone islands.

SUMATRA

MALAY PENINSULA

nern coast of India seas separates it n sea levels were lower.

COLD WILDERNESS

Siberia is a vast wilderness covering most of northern Asia. Its name comes from a Tatar word meaning "sleeping land." Siberia is renowned for its long, almost snowless, bitterly cold winters.

FREEZING COLD

The world's greatest recorded temperature range has been recorded at Verkhoyansk. Temperatures have reached 99°F, and plunged as low as -90°F.

ALASKA

CENTRAL SIBERIAN PLATEAU

⑦

VERKHOYANSKIY KHREBET

Lena

Ob' S I B E R I A

A

STANOVOY KHREBET

YABLONOVYY KHREBET

PIK POBEDY
+ 24,393 ft

①

A L T A I   M O U N T A I N S

Lake Baikal

PLATEAU OF MONGOLIA

IEN SHAN

TARIM BASIN

QILIAN SHAN

G O B I

COLD I

The Gobi is one largest deserts, bu nor sand. It is a desolate, bare

KUNLUN MOUNTAINS
PLATEAU OF TIBET

This is the world's largest mountain plateau with an average height of over 13,600 ft.

Himalayas is a Nepalese word meaning "home of the snows."

GONGGA SHAN
24,790 ft +

ANNAPURNA
26,545 ft +

MOUNT EVEREST
+ 29,029 ft

⊙ Lhasa

H I M A L A Y A S

Over 80 of the worlds 100 highest peaks are found in the Himalayas.

Brahmaputra

Ganges

⑤

E A S T E R N   G H A T S

Calcutta ⊙   MOUTHS OF THE GANGES

Irrawaddy

SHAN

WETTEST PLACE

High monsoon rainfall makes Cherrapunji the world's wettest place with 37 ft 6 in of rain recorded in a year.

G A N G E S   F A N

Ra

⑥

A

ANDAMAN ISLANDS

B A Y   O F   B E N G A L

CYCLONES

Monsoon season in the Bay of Bengal frequently heralds the arrival of tropical cyclones. These intense storms are capable of terrific destruction – particularly in the low-lying Ganges Delta area, which was devastated by cyclones in 1970 and 1991.

+ -6,460 ft

SRI LANKA

⑥ TEARDROP ISLAND

Sri Lanka is a large island lying just off the sout like a giant teardrop. A narrow strait of shallow from the mainland, to which it was joined whe

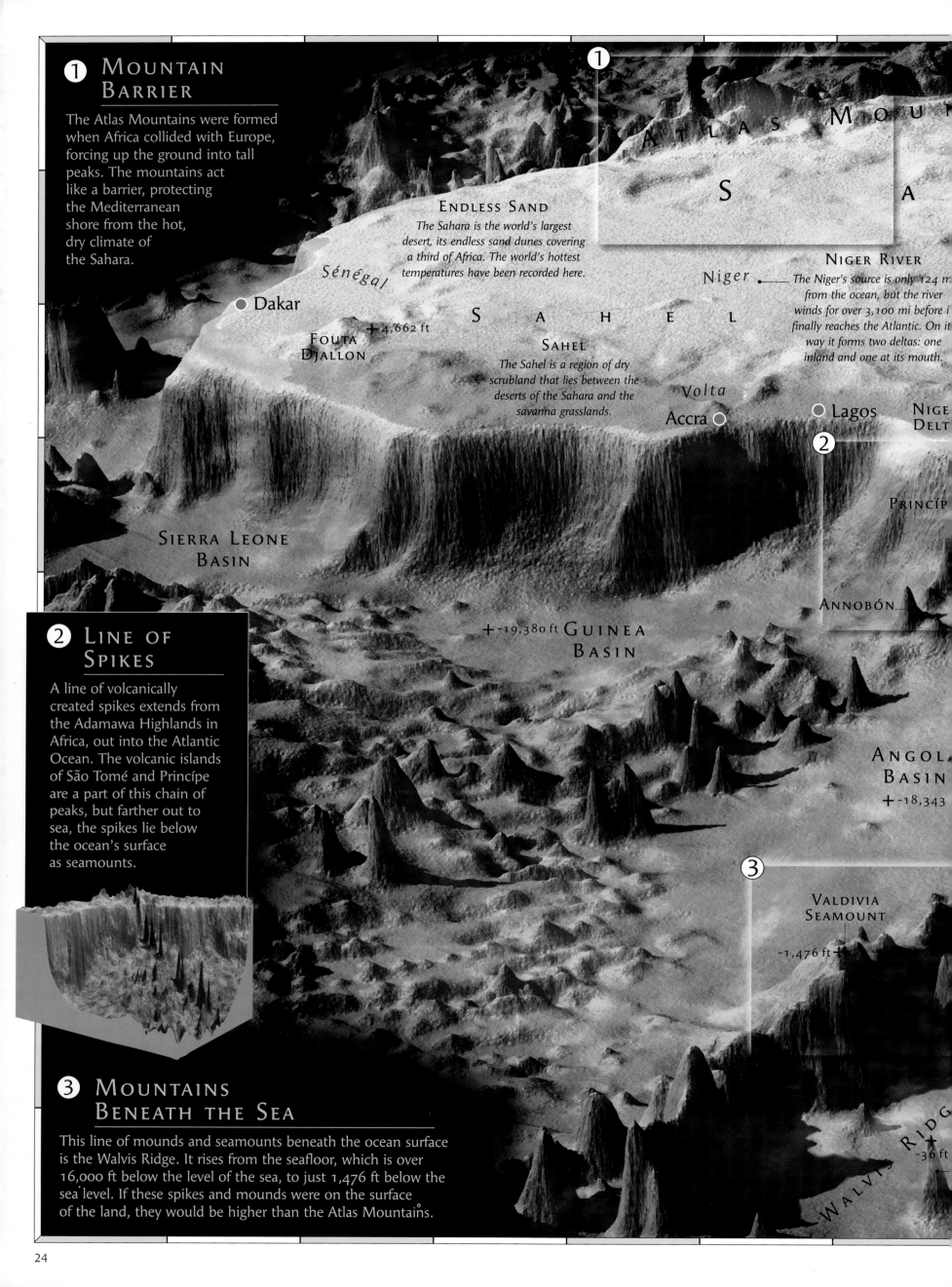

① MOUNTAIN BARRIER

The Atlas Mountains were formed when Africa collided with Europe, forcing up the ground into tall peaks. The mountains act like a barrier, protecting the Mediterranean shore from the hot, dry climate of the Sahara.

ENDLESS SAND

The Sahara is the world's largest desert, its endless sand dunes covering a third of Africa. The world's hottest temperatures have been recorded here.

ATLAS MOU

S

A

NIGER RIVER

The Niger's source is only 124 m from the ocean, but the river winds for over 3,100 mi before i finally reaches the Atlantic. On it way it forms two deltas: one inland and one at its mouth.

Niger

Sénégal

● Dakar

S A H E L

+ 4,662 ft

FOUTA
DJALLON

SAHEL

The Sahel is a region of dry scrubland that lies between the deserts of the Sahara and the savanna grasslands.

Volta

Accra ○

○ Lagos

NIGE
DELT

SIERRA LEONE
BASIN

PRINCÍP

ANNOBÓN

+ -19,380 ft GUINEA
BASIN

② LINE OF SPIKES

A line of volcanically created spikes extends from the Adamawa Highlands in Africa, out into the Atlantic Ocean. The volcanic islands of São Tomé and Princípe are a part of this chain of peaks, but farther out to sea, the spikes lie below the ocean's surface as seamounts.

ANGOLA
BASIN

+ -18,343

③

VALDIVIA
SEAMOUNT

-1,476 ft +

③ MOUNTAINS BENEATH THE SEA

This line of mounds and seamounts beneath the ocean surface is the Walvis Ridge. It rises from the seafloor, which is over 16,000 ft below the level of the sea, to just 1,476 ft below the sea level. If these spikes and mounds were on the surface of the land, they would be higher than the Atlas Mountains.

-36 ft

WALVIS RIDG

Africa

AFRICA IS AN ANCIENT, ERODED CONTINENT. It has few large mountain ranges, and its surface is blanketed with vast deserts and dense rainforests. The Great Rift Valley runs like a scar across the landscape in the east, and is made up of deep valleys and jagged, volcanic peaks.

REGIONS OF AFRICA

MAIN VEGETATION ZONES

- ☐ Desert
- ☐ Lowlands
- ◼ Mountains
- ◼ Rainforest
- ☐ Savanna

INCREDIBLE FACTS

▲ **Highest point**
Kilimanjaro, Tanzania
19,340 ft above sea level

▼ **Lowest point**
Lake 'Assal, Djibouti
512 ft below sea level

● **Hottest place**
Al 'Azïzïyah, Libya
Max. temperature 136°F

● **Coldest place**
Ifrane, Morocco
Min. temperature −11°F

Deserts cover huge portions of Africa. The Sahara covers a third of the continent.

The Atlas Mountains are one of Africa's few mountain ranges.

Plentiful rainfall in the Congo Basin allows lush vegetation to grow.

Between the rainforests and the deserts are vast plains of dusty savanna grassland.

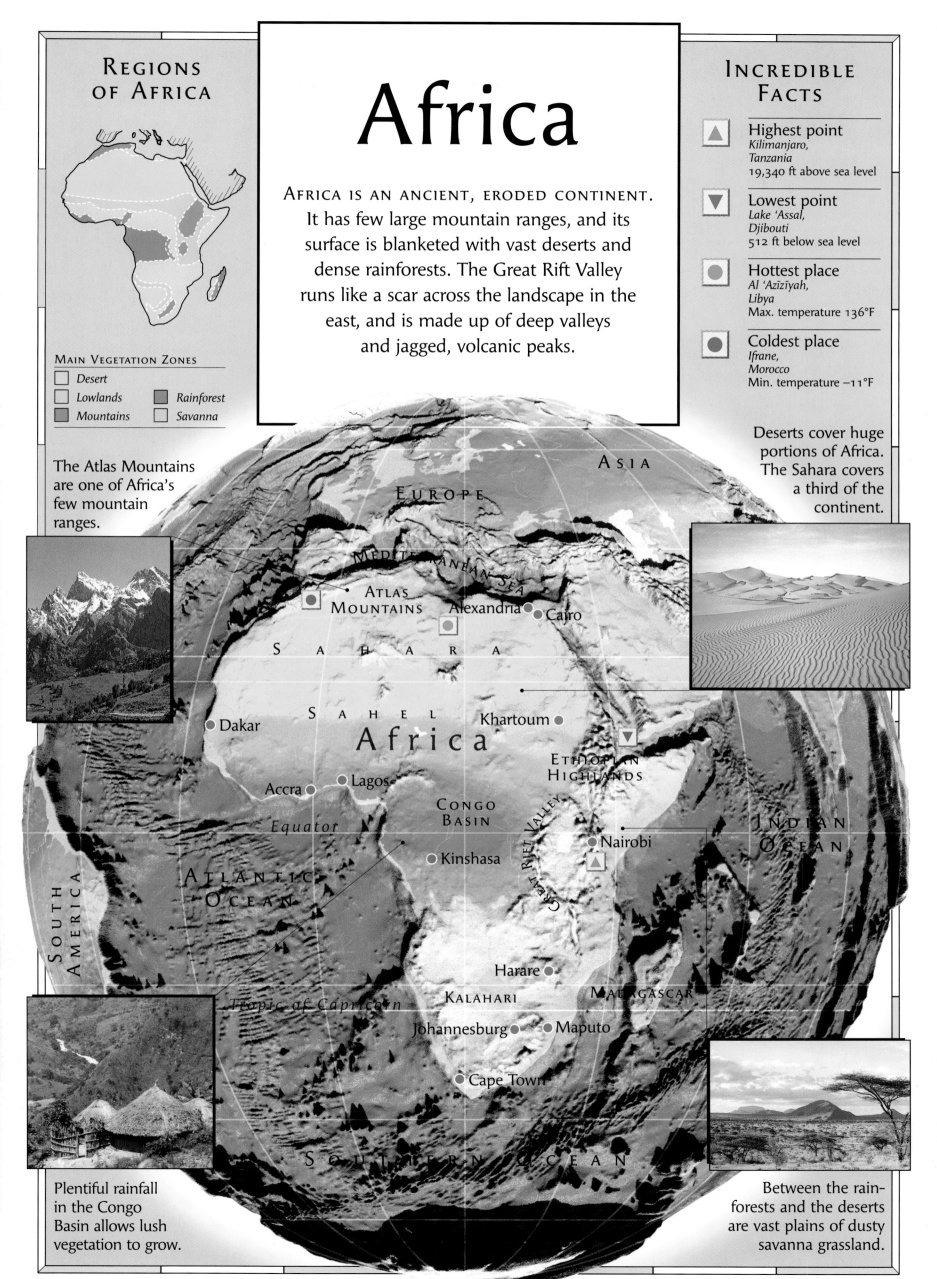

ASIA

EUROPE

MEDITERRANEAN SEA

ATLAS MOUNTAINS

Alexandria · Cairo

SAHARA

SAHEL

· Dakar

Khartoum ·

Africa

ETHIOPIAN HIGHLANDS

Accra · · Lagos

CONGO BASIN

Equator

· Kinshasa

Nairobi

ATLANTIC OCEAN

GREAT RIFT VALLEY

INDIAN OCEAN

SOUTH AMERICA

Harare ·

MADAGASCAR

Tropic of Capricorn

KALAHARI

Johannesburg · · Maputo

· Cape Town

SOUTHERN OCEAN

6 ROCKY SPIRES

The isolated, rocky Tibesti mountains in the middle of the Sahara desert were formed by "hot spots" of volcanic activity. Molten rocks forced their way through the ground and solidified into craggy peaks.

Africa

6,100 mi

4,100 mi

Atlantic Ocean

Indian Ocean

SEA

ARABIAN PENINSULA

RAS DASHEN TERARA 15,157 ft

ETHIOPIAN HIGHLANDS

HORN OF AFRICA

OGADEN

KIRINYAGA 17,060 ft

KILIMANJARO 19,341 ft

LAKE VICTORIA

Source of the Nile

Nairobi

GREAT RIFT VALLEY

ANCIENT REMAINS

remains of early
ns Homo habilis
been found here,
ones and primitive
ements have been
ed at 2.5 million
years old.

Dar es Salaam

SOMALI BASIN

COMOROS

AMIRANTE ISLANDS

RIDGE

4

MADAGASCAR

LAKE NYASA

arare

Zambezi

DRAKENSBERG

The Drakensberg are part of a ring of
mountains that surrounds the southern
tip of Africa. They form a rocky rim
that plunges down to the flat coastal
plains in a series of cliffs.

Maputo

BASSAS DA INDIA

ZAMBEZI CANYON

ZAMBEZI FAN

NATAL VALLEY

MOZAMBIQUE PLATEAU

MADAGASCAR PLATEAU

-16,736 ft

NATAL BASIN

5 CRACKS IN THE EARTH

The Great Rift Valley runs like two huge scars across east Africa, encircling Lake Victoria, and bounded by mountainous plateaus. The flat-bottomed valley was formed when stresses deep within the Earth caused it to crack apart.

4 SPLIT APART

Madagascar is the world's fourth biggest island. It is a large chunk of Africa that split off from the mainland 80 million years ago. The island's isolation has allowed many unique species of plants and animals to evolve.

The world's highest sand dunes are found in the Sahara at Isaouane-N-Tifernine, central Algeria. The dunes here have reached heights of 1,526 ft. ⑥

MEDITERRANEAN SEA

A I N S

H A H A G G A R

MASSIF DE L'AIR

LAKE CHAD
is a remnant of an ancient inland sea. It is still steadily shrinking today.

EMI KOUSSI
11,204 ft +

TIBESTI

S A H A R A

LIBYAN DESERT

DARFUR

● **Cairo**
is Africa's largest city; almost seven million people live here.

THE RIVER NILE
The Nile is the world's longest river. It flows 4,145 mi forming a large delta on the Mediterranean Sea.

Nile

RED

NUBIAN DESERT

● Khartou...

JOS PLATEAU

ADAMAWA HIGHLANDS

CAMEROON MOUNTAIN

ISLA DE BIOCO

SÃO TOMÉ

CONGO FAN

MASSIF DES BONGO

Ubangi

Congo

CONGO BASIN
In the center of Africa is a broad, shallow depression through which the mighty Congo river flows. Although it is the main route inland, there are many waterfalls and rapids along the river's length, which makes it very difficult to navigate.

○ Kinshasa

BIÉ PLATEAU

SUDD ⑤

MITUMBA RANGE

GREAT RIFT VALLEY

V...
The s...
An...
*Th...
hu...
ha...
The
imp...
da...*

VICTORIA FALLS
Where the Zambezi River flows over this rocky escarpment, dramatic waterfalls and a deep canyon have formed.

HUILA PLATEAU

KALAHARI DESERT
The Kalahari is Africa's great southern desert. It lies in a shallow depression known as the Kalahari basin. The sand in the Kalahari is a vivid color, caused by iron oxides in the surrounding rocks.

N A M I B   D E S E R T

SKELETON COAST
Treacherous shoals and shallow seas off the coast of Namibia have caused many shipwrecks, giving this part of the African coast the name the "Skeleton Coast."

GHAAP PLATEAU

GROOT KARASBERGE

Orange River

Johannesburg ●

PHOFUNG
+ 10,767 ft

CAPE BASIN

VEMA SEAMOUNT

ORANGE FAN

Cape Town ●

AGULHAS BANK

GREAT KAROO

D R A K E N S B E R G

1 MOUNTAIN SPINE

1 MOUNTAIN SPINE

A ridge of high mountains form the backbone of New Guinea, the world's second largest island. At the eastern tip, the mountains split into two arms, divided by the deep New Britain Trench. New Guinea was once part of Australia, but became physically separated when the sea flooded into the Torres Strait, about 8000 years ago.

PHILIPPINES BASIN

BORNEO

JAVA

TIMOR

SAHUL SHELF

Darwin ○
was almost totally
destroyed in 1974 by a
tropical cyclone.

ARNHEM
LAND

KIMBERLEY
PLATEAU

TANAMI
DESERT

JAVA RIDGE

GREAT SANDY
DESERT

MACDONNELL
RANGES

Alice Springs ●

ROO
RISE

GIBSON DESERT
The Gibson Desert is named after Alfred
Gibson, a member of the first European
expedition to cross the desert, who
was lost while searching for water.

ULURU
Uluru (Ayers Rock) is a massive
sandstone outcrop. It is a sacred si
for the Aboriginal native peoples.

HAMERSLEY
RANGE

EXMOUTH PLATEAU

OUTBACK
West of the Great Dividing Range is
the area known to Australians as the
Inland, or the Outback. It is largely
desert scrub and immense stretches
remain completely uninhabited.

GREAT VICTORIA
DESERT

NULLARBOR PLAIN

The Nullarbor Plain is a
low-lying limestone platea
that is so flat that the
Trans-Australian Railway
runs through it in a straigh
line for over 250 mi.

DARLING RANGE

○ Perth
is one of the
world's most
isolated major
cities. It is over
2500 mi away
from the large
cities on Australia's
eastern coast.

GUM TREES
Eucalyptus trees (also known as gum trees
or stringybark trees) are found throughout
Australia. Their leaves contain eucalyptus oil,
which makes them highly flammable during
the dry season, when bush fires are common.

CUVIER
PLATEAU

2 TASMANIA

Tasmania lies 150 mi
south of the Australian
mainland. Physically
it is the southern tip of
Australia's only mountain
chain, the Great Dividing
Range. It became separated
from Australia by rising sea
levels at the end of the last
Ice Age, 18,000 years ago.

+ -6,463 ft
NATURALISTE
PLATEAU

SOUTH A

DEEP WATER
The southern coasts of Australia lie relativ
close to the edge of the continental shelf
The sea floor drops away rapidly to the
depths of the South Australian Basin.

Australasia & Oceania

THE MYRIAD OF SMALL ISLANDS dotted across the Pacific Ocean and the large landmass of Australia form the Earth's most fragmented continent. Australia is flat, stable and largely desert, while many of the surrounding islands are rugged and volcanically active, lying around the edge of the Pacific "Ring of Fire."

INCREDIBLE FACTS

▲ **Highest point**
Mount Wilhelm,
Papua New Guinea
14,793 ft above sea level

▼ **Lowest point**
Lake Eyre,
Australia
52 ft below sea level

● **Hottest place**
Bourke,
Australia
Max. temperature 127°F

● **Coldest place**
Canberra,
Australia
Min. temperature –8°F

MAIN VEGETATION ZONES

☐ Desert   ☐ Grassland
■ Forest   ☐ Mediterranean

Tropical rainforests grow across the northern tip of Australia and over eastern New Guinea.

Many islands across the Pacific are fringed by coral reefs.

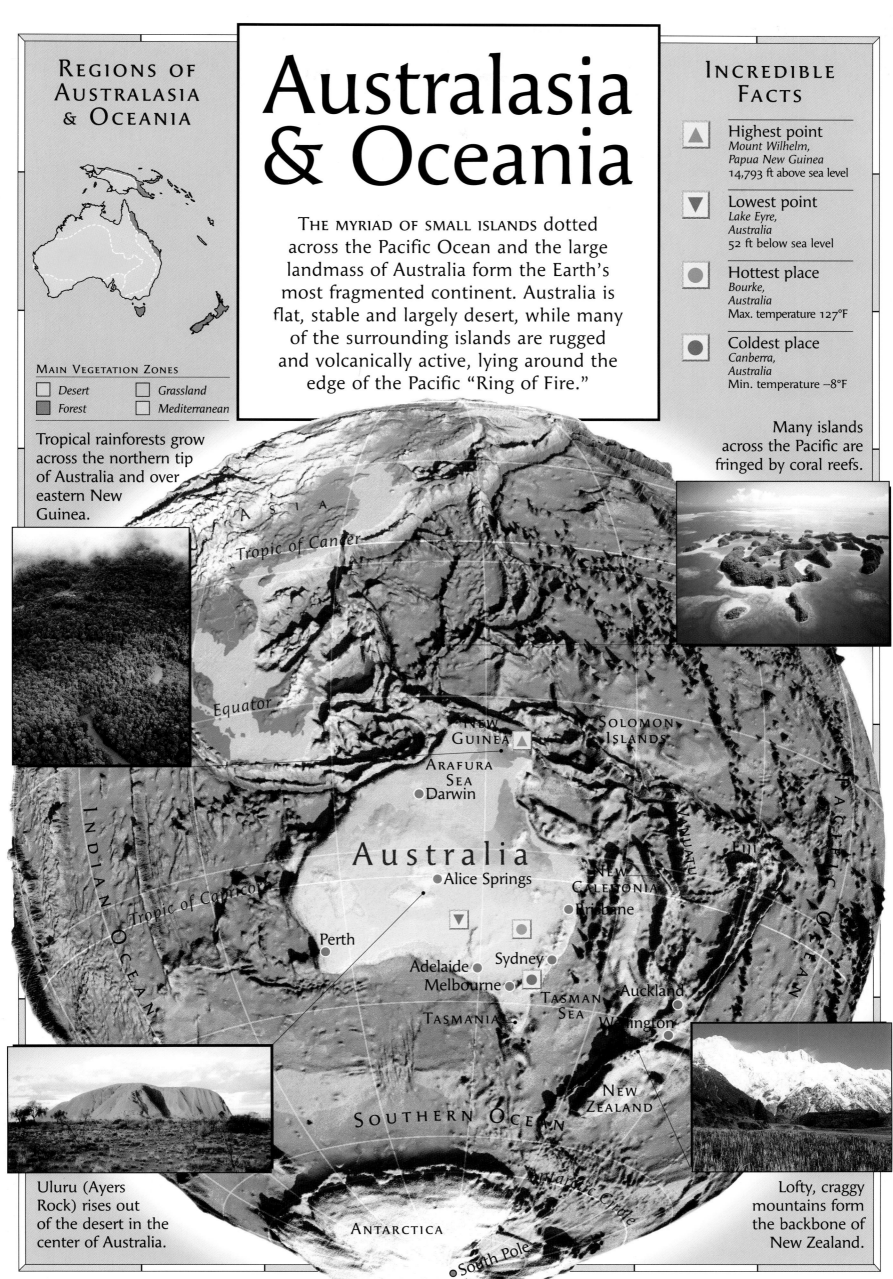

Uluru (Ayers Rock) rises out of the desert in the center of Australia.

Lofty, craggy mountains form the backbone of New Zealand.

Fiji has been formed by volcanoes, as have most of the islands in the Pacific. On Fiji's islands, high volcanic peaks tower above the palm-fringed beaches, which have become a magnet for tourists.

Australasia & Oceania

11,000 mi

5,800 mi

Indian Ocean

Pacific Ocean

ANTARCTICA

ALL ISLAND

E I A

ANESIAN ASIN

+ 14,872 ft

NAURU

PHOENIX ISLAND

N

5,341 ft

VANUATU A

NEW CALEDONIA

NORFOLK RIDGE

NORTH FIJI BASIN

NORFOLK ISLAND

FIJI

LAU BASIN

⑤

NEW CALEDONIA BASIN

LAU RIDGE

TONGA TRENCH

ORD HOWE RISE

NEW HEBRIDES TRENCH

SOUTH FIJI BASIN

④

OZBOURN SEAMOUNT

Auckland

MOUNT RUAPEHU
+9,177 ft

③

NORTH ISLAND

MOUNT COOK
+12,349 ft

Wellington

NEW ZEALAND

KERMADEC TRENCH

Christchurch

SOUTH ISLAND

CHATHAM RISE

③ RUGGED LAND

New Zealand is green, rugged, and mountainous. Beneath the land is a plate boundary, where two parts of the Earth's crust meet. This causes volcanoes, boiling mud pools, and steam geysers, especially on North Island.

④ OCEAN DEPTHS

The Kermadec and Tonga ocean trenches form a vast underwater valley running northeast from New Zealand to Fiji. The eastern ocean floor is plunging down beneath the western floor. The energy generated by this action produces immense heat. Above the trench, a long undersea ridge has been created, which occasionally breaks the surface as volcanic islands.

PALAU

CAROLINE ISLANDS

MARSH

PUNCAK JAYA
+16,535 ft ①

+14,793 ft
MOUNT WILHELM

NEW GUINEA

NEW BRITAIN

NEW BRITAIN
TRENCH

ONTONG JAVA
RISE

SOLOMON ISLANDS

M

C

MEL

RAFURA
SHELF

METAL ORES

*Some of the world's largest
deposits of bauxite, used
to make aluminum,
are found here.*

TORRES STRAIT

CAPE YORK
PENINSULA

*When the Cape York Peninsula was
linked to New Guinea, it provided a
gateway for the first nomadic tribes to
enter Australia, over 50,000 years ago.*

GREAT BARRIER REEF

*The Great Barrier Reef is the world's
largest coral reef and the largest living
structure on Earth. It is over 1,200 mi long
and may be as old as 5 million years.*

MOUNT STEWART
+3,271 ft

BARKLY TABLELAND

GREAT DIVIDING RANGE

*The Great Dividing Range is a misleading
name for the mountains in this part of
Australia. Here, they are much lower and
more poorly defined than farther s*

Brisbane

IMPSON
DESERT

GREAT
ARTESIAN
BASIN

*The Great Artesian Basin is a natural
underground source of water that lies under
almost one-fifth of Australia. It is a vital
resource in a continent that suffers
from severe water shortages.*

DARLING DOWNS

*This area is known as the
"Breadbasket of Australia"
because of the amount of
cereal crops grown here.*

LAKE EYRE
BASIN

Darling

FLINDERS
RANGES

Murray

MOUNT
KOSCIUSKO
+7,310 ft

Sydney
*is Australia's
largest city.
It is located on
a spectacular
natural harbor.*

GREAT DIVIDING RANGE

LORD HOWE SEAMOUNTS

LORI
HOW
ISLAN

SPENCER
GULF

Adelaide

KANGAROO
ISLAND

② GREAT DIVIDING RANGE

Melbourne

BASS STRAIT

TASMANIA

TASMAN PLAIN

+305 ft

GASCOYNE
TABLEMOUNT

TRALIAN BASIN
+-19,193 ft

EAST
TASMAN
PLATEAU

+-2,165 ft

TASMAN
LATEAU

TASMAN
BASIN

FREEZING WEATHER

Antarctica is renowned for its extreme weather. High winds scour the surface of the ice cap, making temperatures even lower. The seas surrounding Antarctica are also some of the stormiest in the world. Mountainous seas, icebergs, and almost continual gale force winds make navigation very difficult.

ARGENTINE BASIN

NORTH SCOTIA RIDGE

①

SOUTH GEORGIA

SOUTH SANDWICH ISLANDS

ISLAS ORCADAS SEAMOUNT

PALMER LAND

SOUTH SCOTIA RIDGE

RONNE ICE SHELF

ANTARCTIC PENINSULA

ADELAIDE ISLAND

ALEXANDER ISLAND

VINSON MASSIF
+ 16,066 ft

ELLSWORTH MOUNTAINS

COLD DESERT

Antarctica has the lowest precipitation of any of the Earth's continents. In some places there are dry valleys where it has not rained for two million years. These valleys are thought to be Earth's nearest equivalent to the surface of Mars.

ELLSWORTH LAND

LESSER ANTARCTICA

MARIE BYRD LAND

MOUNT SIDLEY
13,717 ft +

PETER I ISLAND

THURSTON ISLAND

MOUNT SIPLE
10,171 ft +

BELLINGSHAUSEN PLAIN

MARIE BYRD SEAMOUNT

ANTARCTIC TREATY

No one country owns Antarctica, although several claim portions of the continent. In 1961, the Antarctic Treaty set aside Antarctica for nonpolitical scientific investigation.

AMUNDSEN PLAIN

① ROCKY RIDGES

The rocky Antarctic Peninsula stretches 800 mi northward from Antarctica toward South America. The peninsula's spiky peaks were formed at the same time as the Andes. An undersea range, the Scotia Ridge, marks the continuation of the mountains underwater. One of the first recorded sightings of Antarctica was of this area, in 1820 by Edward Branfield.

② ICE SHELF

The Ross Ice Shelf is an immense pack of ice, covering 200,000 sq mi, almost the size of France. It is the world's largest floating body of ice, and it is continually changing its size and shape. Glaciers flow down from the heart of the continent to feed the ice shelf, and at its outer edge, chunks of ice are constantly breaking off to form icebergs.

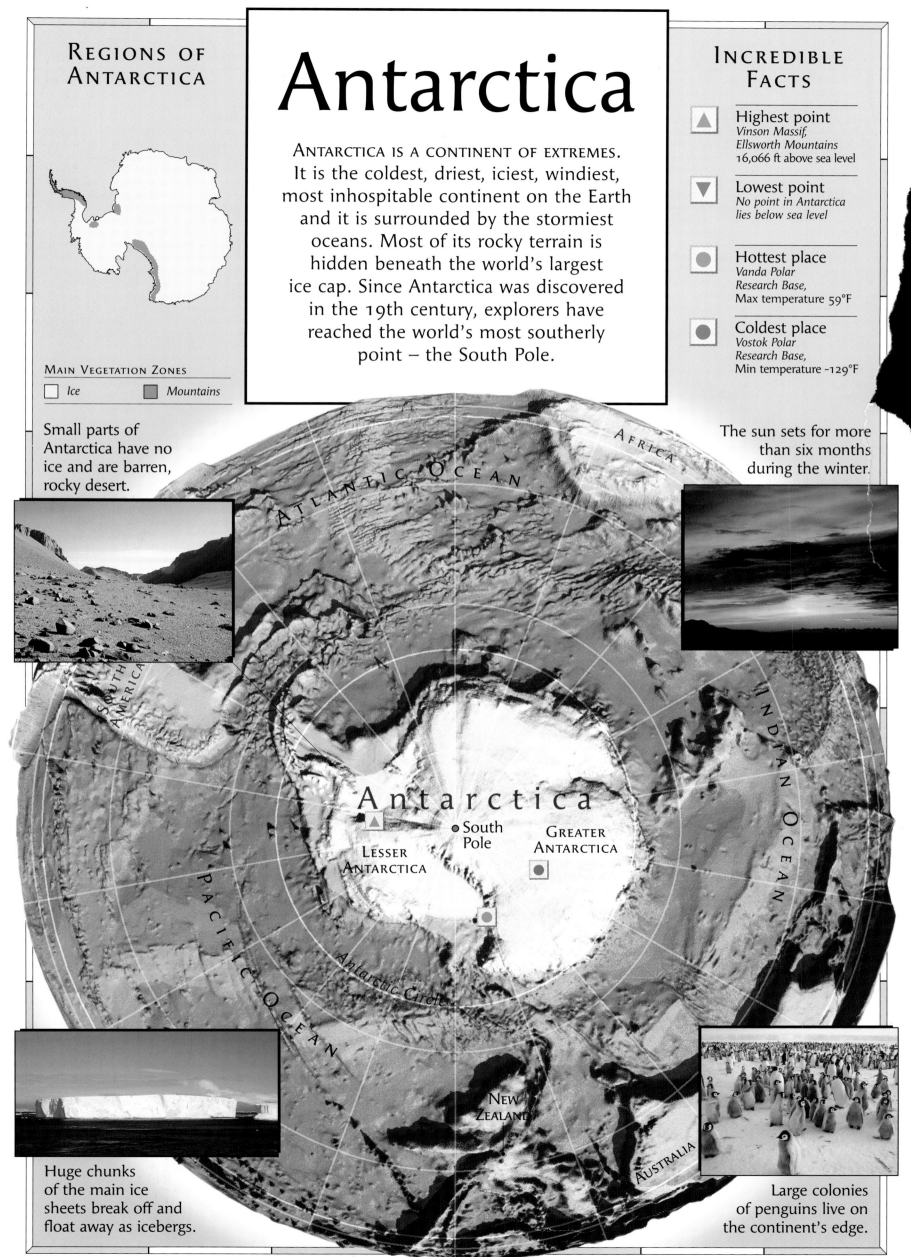

REGIONS OF ANTARCTICA

MAIN VEGETATION ZONES

☐ Ice   ■ Mountains

Small parts of Antarctica have no ice and are barren, rocky desert.

Antarctica

ANTARCTICA IS A CONTINENT OF EXTREMES. It is the coldest, driest, iciest, windiest, most inhospitable continent on the Earth and it is surrounded by the stormiest oceans. Most of its rocky terrain is hidden beneath the world's largest ice cap. Since Antarctica was discovered in the 19th century, explorers have reached the world's most southerly point – the South Pole.

INCREDIBLE FACTS

▲ Highest point
Vinson Massif, Ellsworth Mountains
16,066 ft above sea level

▼ Lowest point
No point in Antarctica lies below sea level

● Hottest place
Vanda Polar Research Base,
Max temperature 59°F

● Coldest place
Vostok Polar Research Base,
Min temperature -129°F

The sun sets for more than six months during the winter.

Huge chunks of the main ice sheets break off and float away as icebergs.

ATLANTIC OCEAN · SOUTH AMERICA · AFRICA · INDIAN OCEAN · PACIFIC OCEAN

Antarctica

● South Pole

LESSER ANTARCTICA · GREATER ANTARCTICA

Antarctic Circle

NEW ZEALAND · AUSTRALIA

Large colonies of penguins live on the continent's edge.

R OF ICE

is the world's largest valley
...ter of the ice mass from the
...eet. The glacier flows like a
...50 mi, and when it reaches
...it is almost 125 mi wide.

KEMP
LAND

MOUNT
ELKINS
7,546 ft

LACIER

PRINCESS
ELIZABETH LAND

+13,222 ft
ice thickness
3,412 ft

R
...TICA

Antarctica contains 90% of the
world's ice, and thus most of
the Earth's fresh water reserves.
The vast Antarctic ice dome
rises steeply from the coast and
is thickest in Greater Antarctica.
If all the ice melted, sea levels would
rise globally by as much as 210 ft.

ICE THICKNESS

☐	1,600 ft
☐	3,300 ft
☐	5,000 ft
☐	6,600 ft
☐	8,200 ft
☐	9,800 ft
☐	11,500⁺ft

5,800 mi
Antarctica
3,800 mi

Pacific
Ocean

AUSTRALASIA
& OCEANIA

WILHELM II LAND

ENDERBY
PLAIN

BANZARE
SEAMOUNT
+ -610 ft

KERGUELEN
PLATEAU

WORLD'S LOWEST TEMPERATURE

Antarctica is by far the coldest continent. In June
1983, the world's lowest temperature of -129°F
was recorded here, at Vostok Polar Research Station.

...AKE

...e ice cap is
...ake 140 mi
...overed by
... been sealed
...s or more.

METEORITE STRIKE

Thousands of meteorites and fragments
of rock have been found embedded in
Antarctica. When the meteorites land,
they become frozen into the ice and can
remain that way for millions of years.

WILKES LAND

LAW
DOME

PETERSEN
BANK

... LAND

MARINE LIFE

The deep oceans surrounding Antarctica are
teeming with a wide variety of marine life.
The great quantities of minute, shrimplike
creatures called krill support much of
the extensive marine food chain.

...ITED LAND

...ive on Antarctica are
...mmentalists. They live
...ucted research bases.

④ ROCKY
SPINE

The Transantarctic Mountains
cut across the center of the
continent for 3,000 mi, in a
series of jagged, frozen peaks.
In many places, the mountains
are engulfed by the great
Antarctic ice sheet and only
isolated peaks, known as
nunataks, poke through the ice.

③ EREBUS

Mount Erebus is the largest of four volcanoes
on Ross Island, at the edge of the vast Ross
Ice Shelf. It is the world's most southerly
active volcano, erupting almost every year
during the 1970s. In 1984, it violently
ejected clouds of gas and lava.

GUNNERUS RIDGE

DRONNING MAUD LAND

ENDERBY LAND

RIVE[R]

The Lambert Glacier
glacier, draining a qua[rter]
main Antarctic ice sh[eet]
slow ice river for over 2[...]
the ice shelves by the sea[...]

LAMBERT G[LACIER]

THICK ICE
The Antarctic ice sheet reaches a maximum thickness
of 15,669 ft, and the great weight of the ice has
pushed down the land beneath it. The ice is so heavy
that it actually deforms the shape of the Earth,
causing it to flatten slightly at the South Pole.

+12,566 ft
ice thickness
9,803 ft

PENGUINS
Almost half of the world's 18 species of
penguins live on Antarctica. They are protected
from the severe weather by layers of fat.
Emperor penguins are the largest of all penguins
and breed solely on the Antarctic ice.

PENSACOLA MOUNTAINS

● South Pole

④

RACE FOR THE POLE
Explorers first tried to reach the South Pole at the
beginning of the 20th century. The race to reach the Pole
was won by a Norwegian, Roald Amundsen, who reached
it on December 14th, 1911. The ill-fated Scott expedition
reached the South Pole a month later, but the
party perished from cold on the return journey.

⑤

MOUNT KIRKPATRICK
+14,856 ft
+14,275 ft
MOUNT MARKHAM

MOUNT McCLINTOCK
+11,457 ft

GREATE[R]
ANTARCTI[C]

MOUNT LISTER
+13,209 ft

TRANSANTARCTIC MOUNTAINS

VICTORIA LAND

②
ROOSEVELT ISLAND

③

ROSS ICE SHELF

MOUNT EREBUS
12,448 ft +

UNDERGROUND L[AKE]
About 2 mi below the surface of th[e]
Lake Vostok, a huge underground [...]
long and 30 mi wide. It was disc[overed by]
scientists in 1996 and it may have [...]
beneath the ice for a million year[s]

ROSS ISLAND

+13,658 ft
MOUNT MINTO

OATES LAND

GEORGE V [LAND]

PENNELL BANK

ISELIN BANK

BALLENY ISLANDS

UNINHA[BITED]
Most people who [...]
scientists and envir[...]
in specially consti[...]

SCOTT SEAMOUNTS

BALLENY SEAMOUNTS

① ICE DOME

Most of Greenland is covered by a huge dome of ice. The weight of the ice has pushed down the land beneath it, in some places by as much as 1,000 ft . If all the ice were scooped out, Greenland would be a flooded rocky basin surrounded by a rim of mountains.

A L A S K A

MOUNT CHAMBERLIN
9,019 ft +

BROOKS RANGE

The Brooks Range is the highest mountain range north of the Arctic Circle.

Mackenzie

PINGOS
Pingos are strange hillocks with cores of ice. They are formed by the freezing and thawing of surface water and are found throughout the Mackenzie Delta.

BANKS
ISLAND

VICTORIA
ISLAND

QUEEN
ELIZABETH
ISLANDS

BARBEAU PEAK
8,543 ft +

ELLESMERE ISLAND

The first expedition to reach the North Pole was led by Robert Peary, setting out from Ellesmere Island in March 1909 and reaching the North Pole one month later.

MELVILLE
PENINSULA

B A F F I N   I S L A N D

KNUD RASMUSSEN

①

BAFFIN BASIN

ICEBERGS
This part of the Arctic is notorious for its icebergs. Huge chunks of the Greenland ice sheet frequently split off and float south towards the Atlantic Ocean as icebergs. It was an iceberg like this that sank the Titanic in 1912.

G R E E N L A N D

G R E E N L A N D

ICE SHEET
The massive ice sheet covering Greenland is the largest in the northern hemisphere, and the world's second largest, after the Antarctic ice sheet.

MOUNT FOREL
11,024 ft +

GUNNBJØRN FJELD
+ 12,139 ft

GREENLAND-
ICELAND RISE

CENTER OF THE EARTH
Snaefellsjokull volcano is the setting for Jules Verne's A Journey to the Center of the Earth.

HVANNADALSHNÚKUR
6,952 ft +

② ON THE RIDGE

Jan Mayen is a craggy, volcanic island that sits above an extension of the Mid-Atlantic Ridge. Here, new land is being created by an upwelling of lava, pushing the two sides of the ridge apart. The island is uninhabited, save for a few people who operate the island's navigation station.

I C E L A N D

Reykavík ○

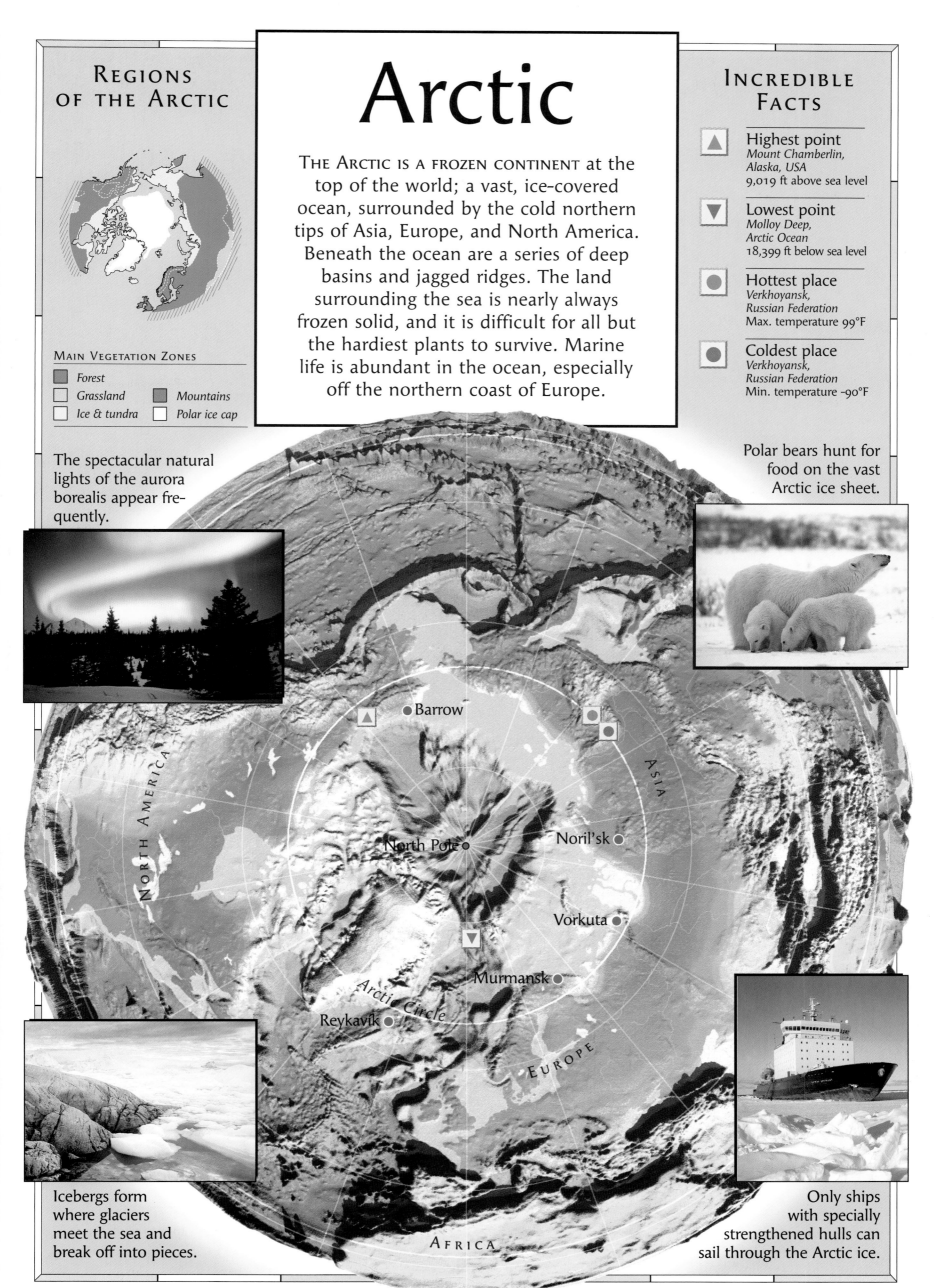

REGIONS OF THE ARCTIC

MAIN VEGETATION ZONES
- ◼ Forest
- ◻ Grassland
- ◻ Ice & tundra
- ◼ Mountains
- ◻ Polar ice cap

Arctic

THE ARCTIC IS A FROZEN CONTINENT at the top of the world; a vast, ice-covered ocean, surrounded by the cold northern tips of Asia, Europe, and North America. Beneath the ocean are a series of deep basins and jagged ridges. The land surrounding the sea is nearly always frozen solid, and it is difficult for all but the hardiest plants to survive. Marine life is abundant in the ocean, especially off the northern coast of Europe.

INCREDIBLE FACTS

▲ **Highest point**
Mount Chamberlin, Alaska, USA
9,019 ft above sea level

▼ **Lowest point**
Molloy Deep, Arctic Ocean
18,399 ft below sea level

● **Hottest place**
Verkhoyansk, Russian Federation
Max. temperature 99°F

● **Coldest place**
Verkhoyansk, Russian Federation
Min. temperature -90°F

The spectacular natural lights of the aurora borealis appear frequently.

Polar bears hunt for food on the vast Arctic ice sheet.

Icebergs form where glaciers meet the sea and break off into pieces.

Only ships with specially strengthened hulls can sail through the Arctic ice.

NORTH AMERICA

ASIA

▲ ● Barrow

North Pole ●

Noril'sk ●

Vorkuta ●

▼

Murmansk ●

Arctic Circle

Reykavik ●

EUROPE

AFRICA

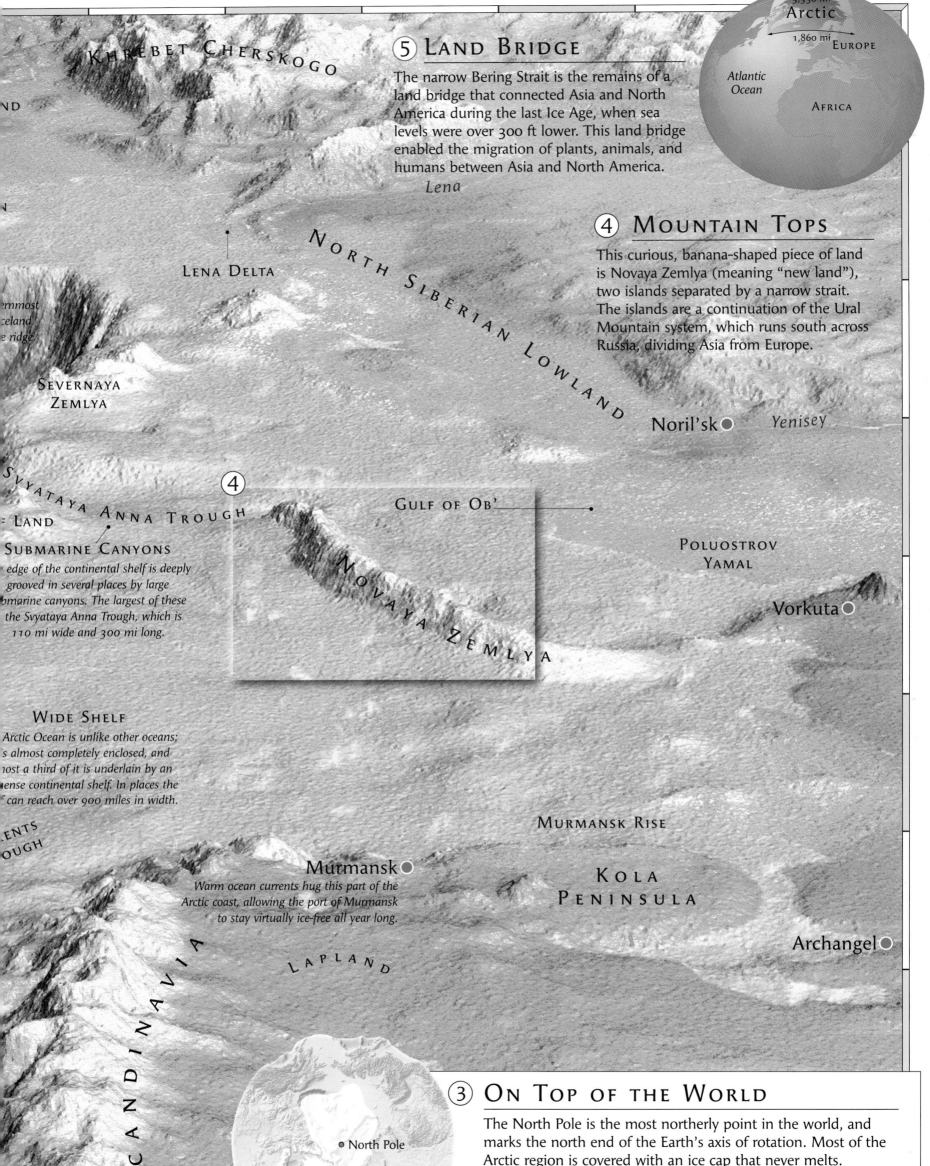

5 LAND BRIDGE

The narrow Bering Strait is the remains of a land bridge that connected Asia and North America during the last Ice Age, when sea levels were over 300 ft lower. This land bridge enabled the migration of plants, animals, and humans between Asia and North America.

Lena

4 MOUNTAIN TOPS

This curious, banana-shaped piece of land is Novaya Zemlya (meaning "new land"), two islands separated by a narrow strait. The islands are a continuation of the Ural Mountain system, which runs south across Russia, dividing Asia from Europe.

KHREBET CHERSKOGO

LENA DELTA

NORTH SIBERIAN LOWLAND

ermost celand e ridge.

SEVERNAYA ZEMLYA

Noril'sk○ *Yenisey*

SVYATAYA ANNA TROUGH

= LAND

4 GULF OF OB'

NOVAYA ZEMLYA

POLUOSTROV YAMAL

SUBMARINE CANYONS

edge of the continental shelf is deeply grooved in several places by large bmarine canyons. The largest of these the Svyataya Anna Trough, which is 110 mi wide and 300 mi long.

Vorkuta○

WIDE SHELF

Arctic Ocean is unlike other oceans; s almost completely enclosed, and ost a third of it is underlain by an iense continental shelf. In places the can reach over 900 miles in width.

MURMANSK RISE

ENTS OUGH

Murmansk○

KOLA PENINSULA

Warm ocean currents hug this part of the Arctic coast, allowing the port of Murmansk to stay virtually ice-free all year long.

Archangel○

SCANDINAVIA

LAPLAND

● North Pole

3 ON TOP OF THE WORLD

The North Pole is the most northerly point in the world, and marks the north end of the Earth's axis of rotation. Most of the Arctic region is covered with an ice cap that never melts. Expeditions trying to reach the North Pole have to cross a vast raft of ice that covers 1,800,000 sq mi and is up to 20 feet thick.

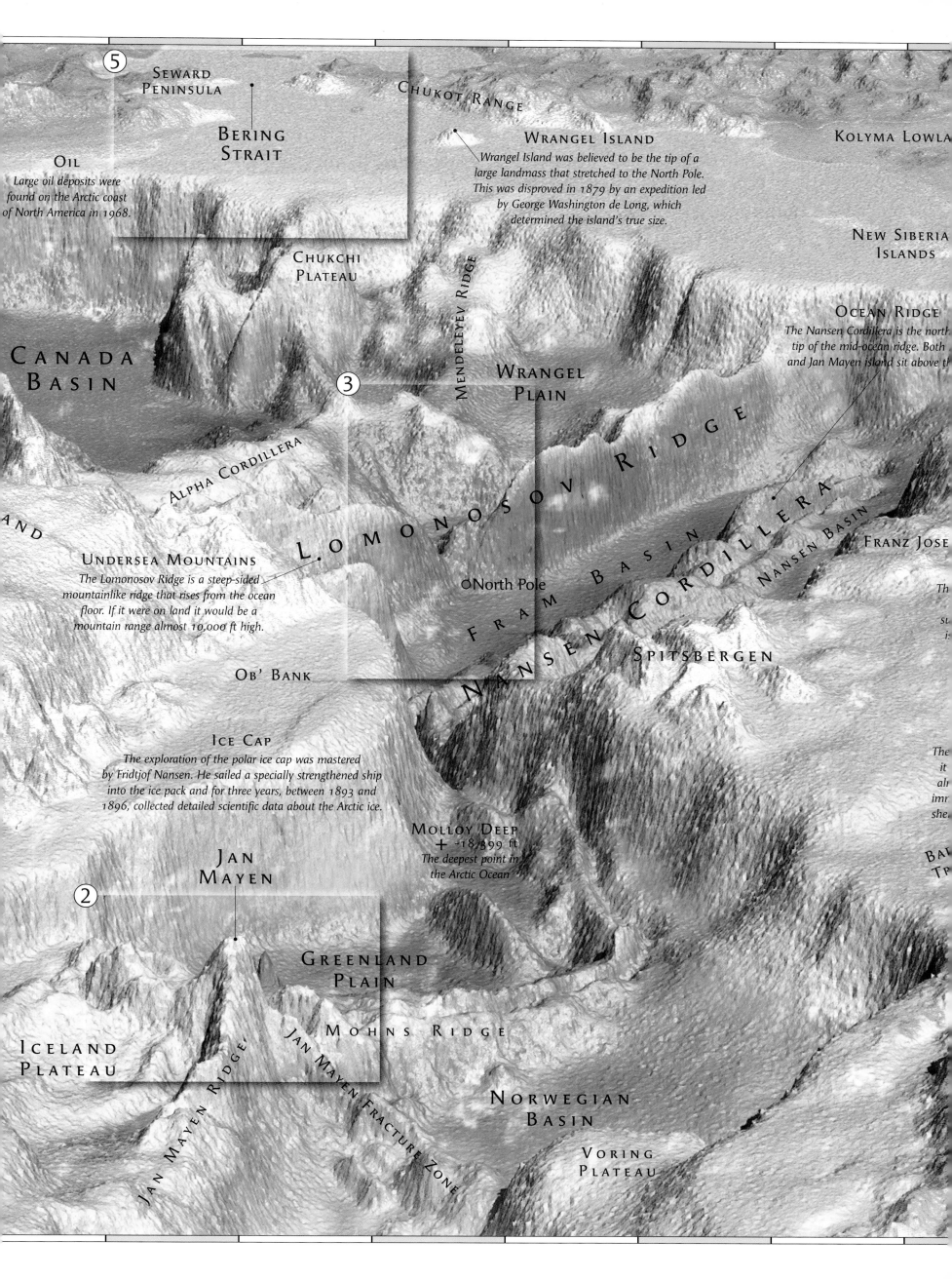

⑤
SEWARD
PENINSULA

CHUKOT RANGE

BERING
STRAIT

WRANGEL ISLAND
*Wrangel Island was believed to be the tip of a
large landmass that stretched to the North Pole.
This was disproved in 1879 by an expedition led
by George Washington de Long, which
determined the island's true size.*

KOLYMA LOWLA

OIL
*Large oil deposits were
found on the Arctic coast
of North America in 1968.*

NEW SIBERIA
ISLANDS

CHUKCHI
PLATEAU

MENDELEYEV RIDGE

WRANGEL
PLAIN

OCEAN RIDGE
*The Nansen Cordillera is the north
tip of the mid-ocean ridge. Both
and Jan Mayen island sit above th*

CANADA
BASIN

③

L O M O N O S O V   R I D G E

ALPHA CORDILLERA

AND

L

NORTH POLE

FRAM BASIN

NANSEN CORDILLERA

NANSEN BASIN

FRANZ JOSE

UNDERSEA MOUNTAINS
*The Lomonosov Ridge is a steep-sided
mountainlike ridge that rises from the ocean
floor. If it were on land it would be a
mountain range almost 10,000 ft high.*

OB' BANK

SPITSBERGEN

Th
su
is

ICE CAP
*The exploration of the polar ice cap was mastered
by Fridtjof Nansen. He sailed a specially strengthened ship
into the ice pack and for three years, between 1893 and
1896, collected detailed scientific data about the Arctic ice.*

The
it
al
imr
she.

MOLLOY DEEP
+ -18,399 ft
*The deepest point in
the Arctic Ocean*

BA
TR

②

JAN
MAYEN

GREENLAND
PLAIN

ICELAND
PLATEAU

JAN MAYEN RIDGE

JAN MAYEN FRACTURE ZONE

MOHNS RIDGE

NORWEGIAN
BASIN

VORING
PLATEAU

INDEX

40

PICTURE CREDITS

Bruce Coleman: H Reinhard 35 br; K Nels Swenson 35 tl; Dr E Pott 39 br; J Johnson 39 tl.
Frank Lane Picture Agency: W Wisniewski 35 bl. *Images of Africa:* D.K. Jones 27 br.
Natural History Picture Agency: M. Wendler 10 tr. *Oxford Scientific Films:* 6 tr; Dr Mike
Hill 35 tr; N Rosing 39 tr. *Pictor:* 31 bl. *Planet Earth Pictures:* Jan T. Johansson 39 tl.
Robert Harding: 6 br; 6 tl; 14 tr; G Renner 27 tr, David Poole 27 bl, C. Tokeley 39 tr.
South American Pictures: Tony Morrison 10 br. *Still Pictures:* R. Seitre 39 tl.
Stock Market: 6 bl; 27 tl; 27 tl. *Tony Stone:* H Strand 10 bl; J Warden 10 tl;
D Johnston 14 br; R.Frerck 14 bl; D Austen 31 tl, 31 bl; P Chesley 31 tr; David Austen
39 br; G. Johnson 39bl. *World Pictures:* 14 tl.

EASTERN HEMISPHERE